Pearson Scott Foresman

Leveled Reader
Teaching Guide

Glenview, Illinois • Boston, Massachusetts • Chandler, Arizona • Upper Saddle River, New Jersey

Accelerated
Reader®

ISBN: 13: 978-0-328-48454-6
ISBN: 10:   0-328-48454-7
10 V016 13

Table of Contents

LEVELED READER TITLE	Instruction	Comprehension Practice	Vocabulary Practice
Mr. Post's Project	12–13	14	15
What's Money All About?	16–17	18	19
Journey Across the Arctic	20–21	22	23
The Road to New York	24–25	26	27
With a Twist	28–29	30	31
All About Penguins	32–33	34	35
Puppy Problems	36–37	38	39
A Family of Collectors	40–41	42	43
The Magic of Coyote	44–45	46	47
Animals of the Concrete Jungle	48–49	50	51
Grape Season	52–53	54	55
Grandmother Spider Steals the Sun	56–57	58	59
Animal Tracking: Learn More About Animals	60–61	62	63
Whales and Other Amazing Animals	64–65	66	67
Coral Reefs	68–69	70	71
Extraordinary Athletes	72–73	74	75
Largest, Fastest, Lightest, Longest	76–77	78	79
Gemstones Around the World	80–81	82	83

Graphic Organizers

Introduction

Scott Foresman *Reading Street* provides more than 750 leveled readers that help children become better readers and build a lifelong love of reading. The *Reading Street* leveled readers are engaging texts that help children practice critical reading skills and strategies. They also provide opportunities to build vocabulary, understand concepts, and develop reading fluency.

The leveled readers were developed to be age-appropriate and appealing to children at each grade level. The leveled readers consist of engaging texts in a variety of genres, including fantasy, folk tales, realistic fiction, historical fiction, and narrative and expository nonfiction. To better address real-life reading skills that children will encounter in testing situations and beyond, a higher percentage of nonfiction texts is provided at each grade.

USING THE LEVELED READERS

You can use the leveled readers to meet the diverse needs of your children. Consider using the readers to

- practice critical skills and strategies
- build fluency
- build vocabulary and concepts
- build background for the main selections in the student book
- provide a variety of reading experiences, e.g., shared, group, individual, take-home, readers' theater

GUIDED READING APPROACH

The *Reading Street* leveled readers are leveled according to Guided Reading criteria by experts trained in Guided Reading. The Guided Reading levels increase in difficulty within a grade level and across grade levels. In addition to leveling according to Guided Reading criteria, the instruction provided in the *Leveled Reader Teaching Guide* is compatible with Guided Reading instruction. An instructional routine is provided for each leveled reader. This routine is most effective when working with individual children or small groups.

MANAGING THE CLASSROOM

When using the leveled readers with individuals or small groups, you'll want to keep the other children engaged in meaningful, independent learning tasks. Establishing independent practice stations throughout the classroom and child routines for these stations can help you manage the rest of the class while you work with individuals or small groups. Practice stations can include listening, phonics, vocabulary, independent reading, and cross-curricular activities. For classroom management, create a work board that lists the stations and which children should be at each station. Provide instructions at each station that detail the tasks to be accomplished. Update the board and alert children when they should rotate to a new station. For additional support for managing your classroom, see the *Reading Street* Practice Stations' *Classroom Management Handbook.*

USING THE LEVELED READER TEACHING GUIDE

The *Leveled Reader Teaching Guide* provides an instruction plan for each leveled reader based on the same instructional routine.

INTRODUCE THE BOOK The Introduction includes suggestions for creating interest in the text by discussing the title and author, building background, and previewing the book and its features.

READ THE BOOK Before students begin reading the book, have them set purposes for reading and discuss how they can use the reading strategy as they read. Determine how you want students in a particular group to read the text, softly or silently, to a specific point or the entire text. Then use the Comprehension Questions to provide support as needed and to assess comprehension.

REVISIT THE BOOK The Reader Response questions provide opportunities for students to demonstrate their understanding of the text, the target comprehension skill, and vocabulary. The Response Options require students to revisit the text to respond to what they've read and to move beyond the text to explore related content.

SKILL WORK The Skill Work box provides instruction and practice for the target skill and strategy and selection vocabulary. Instruction for an alternate comprehension skill allows teachers to provide additional skill instruction and practice for students.

USING THE GRAPHIC ORGANIZERS

Graphic organizers in blackline-master format can be found on pages 132–152. These can be used as overhead transparencies or as student worksheets.

ASSESSING PERFORMANCE

Use the assessment forms that begin on page 6 to make notes about your students' reading skills, use of reading strategies, and general reading behaviors.

MEASURE FLUENT READING (pp. 6–7) Provides directions for measuring a student's fluency, based on words correct per minute (wcpm), and reading accuracy using a running record.

OBSERVATION CHECKLIST (p. 8) Allows you to note the regularity with which students demonstrate their understanding and use of reading skills and strategies.

STUDENT SELF-ASSESSMENT (p. 9) Helps students identify their own areas of strength and areas where they need further work. This form (About My Reading) encourages them to list steps they can take to become better readers and to set goals as readers. Suggest that students share their self-assessment notes with their families so that family members can work with them more effectively to practice their reading skills and strategies at home.

READING STRATEGY ASSESSMENT (p. 10) Provides criteria for evaluating each student's proficiency as a strategic reader.

PROGRESS REPORT (p. 11) Provides a means to track a student's book-reading progress over a period of time by noting the level at which a student reads and his or her accuracy at that level. Reading the chart from left to right gives you a visual model of how quickly a student is making the transition from one level to the next. Share these reports with parents or guardians to help them see how their child's reading is progressing.

Measure Fluent Reading

Taking a Running Record

A running record is an assessment of a student's oral reading accuracy and oral reading fluency. Reading accuracy is based on the number of words read correctly. Reading fluency is based on the reading rate (the number of words correct per minute) and the degree to which a student reads with a "natural flow."

How to Measure Reading Accuracy

1. Choose a grade-level text of about 80 to 120 words that is unfamiliar to the student.
2. Make a copy of the text for yourself. Make a copy for the student or have the student read aloud from a book.
3. Give the student the text and have the student read aloud. (You may wish to record the student's reading for later evaluation.)
4. On your copy of the text, mark any miscues or errors the student makes while reading. See the running record sample on page 7, which shows how to identify and mark miscues.
5. Count the total number of words in the text and the total number of errors made by the student. Note: If a student makes the same error more than once, such as mispronouncing the same word multiple times, count it as one error. Self-corrections do not count as actual errors. Use the following formula to calculate the percentage score, or accuracy rate:

$$\frac{\text{Total Number of Words} - \text{Total Number of Errors}}{\text{Total Number of Words}} \times 100 = \text{percentage score}$$

Interpreting the Results

- A student who reads **95–100%** of the words correctly is reading at an **independent level** and may need more challenging text.
- A student who reads **90–94%** of the words correctly is reading at an **instructional level** and will likely benefit from guided instruction.
- A student who reads **89%** or fewer of the words correctly is reading at a **frustrational level** and may benefit most from targeted instruction with lower-level texts and intervention.

How to Measure Reading Rate (wcpm)

1. Follow Steps 1–3 above.
2. Note the exact times when the student begins and finishes reading.
3. Use the following formula to calculate the number of words correct per minute (wcpm):

$$\frac{\text{Total Number of Words Read Correctly}}{\text{Total Number of Seconds}} \times 60 = \text{words correct per minute}$$

Interpreting the Results

By the end of the year, a third-grader should be reading approximately 110–120 wcpm.

Running Record Sample

Running Record Sample

Dana had recently begun — 4

volunteering at the animal rescue — 9

shelter where her mom worked as a — 16

veterinarian. The shelter was (just) across — 22

the bay from their house. — 27

   Dana was learning many different — 32

jobs at the shelter. She fed the dogs — 40

and cleaned their cages. She played — 46

catch with the dogs in the shelter's — 53

backyard. Dana's favorite /jŏb/ job, however, — 58

was introducing people to the dogs — 64

waiting for adoption. Whenever a dog — 70

found a new home, Dana was especially (sc) — 77

pleased! — 78

   The road to the shelter crossed over — 85

the bay. Dana looked for the boats in the — 93

channel, but there were none. Dana's — 99

mom turned on the radio to ~~listen~~ hear to — 107

the news as they drove. The weather — 114

reporter announced that a blizzard — 119

might hit some parts of the state. — 126

Notations

Accurate Reading
The student reads a word correctly.

Omission
The student omits words or word parts.

Hesitation
The student hesitates over a word, and the teacher provides the word. Wait several seconds before telling the student what the word is.

Mispronunciation/Misreading
The student pronounces or reads a word incorrectly.

Self-correction
The student reads a word incorrectly but then corrects the error. Do not count self-corrections as actual errors. However, noting self-corrections will help you identify words the student finds difficult.

Insertion
The student inserts words or parts of words that are not in the text.

Substitution
The student substitutes words or parts of words for the words in the text.

Running Record Results
Total Number of Words: **126**
Number of Errors: **5**

Reading Time: **64 seconds**

▶ **Reading Accuracy**

$$\frac{126 - 5}{126} \times 100 = 96.032 = 96\%$$

Accuracy Percentage Score: **96%**

▶ **Reading Rate—WCPM**

$$\frac{121}{64} \times 60 = 113.44 = 113 \text{ words correct per minute}$$

Reading Rate: **113 WCPM**

Observation Checklist

Student's Name _____ **Date** _____

Behaviors Observed	Always (Proficient)	Usually (Fluent)	Sometimes (Developing)	Rarely (Novice)
Reading Strategies and Skills				
Uses prior knowledge and preview to understand what book is about				
Makes predictions and checks them while reading				
Uses context clues to figure out meanings of new words				
Uses phonics and syllabication to decode words				
Self-corrects while reading				
Reads at an appropriate reading rate				
Reads with appropriate intonation and stress				
Uses fix-up strategies				
Identifies story elements: character, setting, plot, theme				
Summarizes plot or main ideas accurately				
Uses target comprehension skill to understand the text better				
Responds thoughtfully about the text				
Reading Behaviors and Attitudes				
Enjoys listening to stories				
Chooses reading as a free-time activity				
Reads with sustained interest and attention				
Participates in discussion about books				

General Comments

About My Reading

Name _____ Date _____

1. Compared with earlier in the year, I am enjoying reading

   ☐ more ☐ less ☐ about the same

2. When I read now, I understand

   ☐ more than I used to ☐ about the same as I used to

3. One thing that has helped me with my reading is

   _____

   _____

4. One thing that could make me a better reader is

   _____

   _____

5. Here is one selection or book that I really enjoyed reading:

   _____

   _____

6. Here are some reasons why I liked it:

   _____

   _____

   _____

   _____

   _____

   _____

Reading Strategy Assessment

Student _____ Date _____

Teacher _____

		Proficient	Developing	Emerging	Not showing trait
Building Background Comments:	Previews	☐	☐	☐	☐
	Asks questions	☐	☐	☐	☐
	Predicts	☐	☐	☐	☐
	Activates prior knowledge	☐	☐	☐	☐
	Sets own purposes for reading	☐	☐	☐	☐
	Other:	☐	☐	☐	☐
Comprehension Comments:	Retells/summarizes	☐	☐	☐	☐
	Questions, evaluates ideas	☐	☐	☐	☐
	Relates to self/other texts	☐	☐	☐	☐
	Paraphrases	☐	☐	☐	☐
	Rereads/reads ahead for meaning	☐	☐	☐	☐
	Visualizes	☐	☐	☐	☐
	Uses decoding strategies	☐	☐	☐	☐
	Uses vocabulary strategies	☐	☐	☐	☐
	Understands key ideas of a text	☐	☐	☐	☐
	Other:	☐	☐	☐	☐
Fluency Comments:	Adjusts reading rate	☐	☐	☐	☐
	Reads for accuracy	☐	☐	☐	☐
	Uses expression	☐	☐	☐	☐
	Other:	☐	☐	☐	☐
Connections Comments:	Relates text to self	☐	☐	☐	☐
	Relates text to text	☐	☐	☐	☐
	Relates text to world	☐	☐	☐	☐
	Other:	☐	☐	☐	☐
Self-Assessment Comments:	Is aware of: Strengths	☐	☐	☐	☐
	Needs	☐	☐	☐	☐
	Improvement/achievement	☐	☐	☐	☐
	Sets and implements learning goals	☐	☐	☐	☐
	Maintains logs, records, portfolio	☐	☐	☐	☐
	Works with others	☐	☐	☐	☐
	Shares ideas and materials	☐	☐	☐	☐
	Other:	☐	☐	☐	☐

Progress Report

Student's Name _____

At the top of the chart, record the book title, its grade/unit/week (for example, 1.2.3), and the student's accuracy percentage. See page 6 for measuring fluency, calculating accuracy and reading rates. At the bottom of the chart, record the date you took the running record. In the middle of the chart, make an X in the box across from the level of the student's reading—frustrational level (below 89% accuracy), instructional level (90–94% accuracy), or independent level (95–100% accuracy). Record the reading rate (WCPM) in the next row.

Book Title						
Grade/Unit/Week						
Reading Accuracy Percentage						
LEVEL — **Frustrational** (89% or below)						
Instructional (90–94%)						
Independent (95% or above)						
Reading Rate (WCPM)						
Date						

Mr. Post's Project

SUMMARY The new school year is under way, and one class has a new teacher, Mr. Post. His experience as a summer volunteer inspires him and his students to develop a yearlong community volunteer project through which students offer their time and skills to members of the community.

LESSON VOCABULARY

community	enthusiasm
labor	mural
nonprofit	organization
reporter	sign-up
success	volunteer

INTRODUCE THE BOOK

INTRODUCE THE TITLE AND AUTHOR Discuss with students the title and the author of *Mr. Post's Project*. Ask them to look at the cover illustration and talk about how it might relate to the title. Ask: Who is the man in the illustration, and what is he doing? Why is his name on the chalkboard?

BUILD BACKGROUND Discuss community service and volunteering. Ask: Why do people volunteer? Have you or members of your family volunteered? Have you ever been helped by volunteers?

ELL Ask students to discuss what aspects of starting a new school year are exciting and which are difficult. Ask: How can others help students who are not native English speakers?

PREVIEW/USE TEXT FEATURES Have students preview the book by looking at the illustrations. Encourage students to use the illustrations to predict the story line. Point out the way in which the text on page 20 is set off with a heading. Ask: Why might the author have done this?

READ THE BOOK

SET PURPOSE Have children set a purpose for reading *Mr. Post's Project*. They might be interested in the type of teacher Mr. Post will be or what kinds of students will be in his class. After looking at the illustrations, you might guide students to set a purpose related to learning more about volunteering or how to organize a volunteer project.

STRATEGY SUPPORT: PRIOR KNOWLEDGE Encourage students to discuss any prior experience in organizing an activity. Remind students that their prior knowledge will help them understand the story. Their prior experience as volunteers or working on simple fundraising projects might well help them understand some of the issues involved with organizing a volunteer project that involves an entire class.

COMPREHENSION QUESTIONS

PAGE 5 Why were students curious about Mr. Post? *(It was his first year at the school.)*

PAGE 10 What ideas did Mr. Post's students have for volunteer projects? *(recycling, delivering groceries for the elderly, raking leaves for people who couldn't rake)*

PAGE 13 How was the class project organized? *(On sign-up sheets, students volunteered to do things they had time for and liked to do.)*

PAGES 16–17 What do the photos show? How realistic are they? *(They show the students doing volunteer activities. They are very realistic even though they aren't real photos.)*

PAGE 20 How do nonprofit groups help with community projects to build homes? *(They pay for materials, equipment, and land, and they organize workers.)*

REVISIT THE BOOK

READER RESPONSE

1. Most of the book takes place in the classroom. Mr. Post fits easily into that setting because he is the teacher.
2. Possible responses should demonstrate an understanding of or questions about volunteering.
3. Possible responses: The baseball player showed dedication when he overcame his injury. A dedication was made to the soldiers who served in the war.
4. Possible response: Yes, because I would like to help people in my community.

EXTEND UNDERSTANDING Remind students that *characters* are the people or animals in stories. Since this book focuses largely on the character of Mr. Post, invite students to discuss him. Ask: What kind of person is Mr. Post? How do you know? Would you like Mr. Post to be your teacher? Ask students to describe how they have reached their conclusions about Mr. Post.

RESPONSE OPTIONS

WRITING Invite students to examine the illustrations in the book closely. Assign each illustration to a small group of students, and have each group write a caption that describes what is happening in the picture. Encourage students to write lively captions or dialogue.

WORD WORK Have each student write a story about an imaginary school volunteer project. Each story should include at least six of the vocabulary words.

SOCIAL STUDIES CONNECTION

As a group, have students plan a classroom volunteer project. On the board, write down the steps that students feel must be done to complete the project, from start to finish. Students should consider the needs of the community, interests and skills of students, fundraising, publicity opportunities, and how to celebrate the project's success.

Skill Work

TEACH/REVIEW VOCABULARY

Read aloud the vocabulary words. Ask students to explain words they already know and to look up words they don't know. Have students practice using unfamiliar words in read-aloud sentences.

TARGET SKILL AND STRATEGY

CHARACTER AND SETTING Remind children that good *characters*—the people in a story—and a believable *setting*—where and when a story takes place—make a story come alive for the reader. *Character traits* are qualities that tell about a character's personality. Good readers try to understand how characters feel and why they do the things they do. Have students analyze the character traits of Mr. Post while they are reading. What clues tell the kind of teacher he is? Students should support their statements with clues and details from the book. Ask them how Mr. Post's classroom—the setting—is like their own classroom and how it is different.

PRIOR KNOWLEDGE Tell students that *prior knowledge* is what they know about a given topic, and it comes from their reading and personal experiences. Explain how connecting prior knowledge to a text can help students understand what they read. Read aloud sections of the story, and pause to ask students what it reminds them of. Tell students that they can use their prior knowledge, as well as illustrations, to determine whether a story is a realistic story or a fantasy.

ADDITIONAL SKILL INSTRUCTION

THEME Explain to students that every story has one "big idea" called the *theme*. Instruct students that they can often determine the theme by asking themselves as they read, "What does the writer want me to learn from reading this story?" Tell students that sometimes the theme will be directly stated. Other times, students can look at the actions taken by characters in the story to figure out the theme.

Name _____

Character and Setting

- A **character** is a person who takes part in the events of a story.
- **Character traits** are qualities of a character that tell information about his or her personality.

Directions Fill in the graphic organizer after rereading *Mr. Post's Project*.

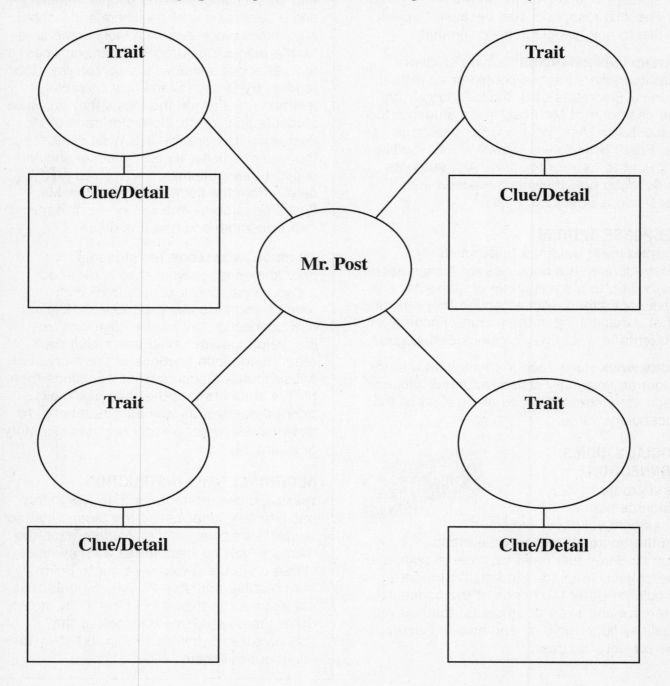

Name _____

Vocabulary

Directions Choose the word from the box that best completes each sentence. Write the word on the line.

> ## Check the Words You Know
>
> ___ community ___ enthusiasm ___ labor ___ mural
> ___ nonprofit ___ organization ___ reporter ___ sign-up
> ___ success ___ volunteer

1. The volunteer _____ helped students plan and buy supplies.

2. The students were so excited, they could not contain their _____ .

3. A _____ gives his or her time to help others.

4. A newspaper _____ visited the surprised students.

5. Many people from the _____ had project ideas for the students.

6. Raking leaves required the students to perform physical _____ .

7. The students made a big _____ to hang on the wall.

8. A _____ organization does not make a profit.

9. Mr. Post hung a _____ sheet on the door so students could volunteer.

10. The community project to clean the park was a huge _____ .

Directions Write a paragraph about volunteering, using as many vocabulary words as you can. Underline each vocabulary word you use.

_____

_____

_____

_____

_____

What's Money All About?

SUMMARY This book gives a lively historical perspective on how and why we began using money. It explains the origins of trading, buying, bargaining, and selling.

LESSON VOCABULARY

bargaining   compromise
currency   mints
wampum

INTRODUCE THE BOOK

INTRODUCE THE TITLE AND AUTHOR Discuss with students the title and the author of *What's Money All About?* Based on the title and the cover illustrations, ask students to describe what they imagine this book will be about. Ask students if they can identify any of the kinds of money on the cover.

BUILD BACKGROUND Ask students to discuss how they get money for the things they want and how they use their money once they have it. Discuss the different kinds of money, such as coins, bills, and checks. Ask students which kind of money is easier for them to handle, which kind is safest, and which kind is more valuable to them.

PREVIEW/USE TEXT FEATURES Have students look at the chapter headings and the illustrations and discuss how these text elements help organize the information in the book. Ask students how the chapter headings help them predict what this book is about.

READ THE BOOK

SET PURPOSE Have students set a purpose for reading *What's Money All About?* Students' curiosity about how money came about or their interest in having their own money should guide this purpose. If students are interested, suggest that they later do research on the different kinds of money in the world.

STRATEGY SUPPORT: SUMMARIZE As students read about bartering and how our system of money began, prompt them to summarize. Summarizing will help students zero in on the most important points in the book. Suggest that students take notes as they read the story, writing down what they consider to be the key points.

COMPREHENSION QUESTIONS

PAGE 7 What is the major problem that arises when people barter? *(Sometimes people cannot agree on the value of goods.)*

PAGE 13 What is the benefit of a coin-based system of money? *(Coins are small and easy to carry.)*

PAGE 15 What was the sequence of events in the development of money during colonial times and the early days of independence? *(The colonies used British pounds; the country needed its own money; Congress began making money so the states could trade with each other more easily.)*

PAGE 16 How many mints are in the United States and which kinds make coins for the marketplace? *(four; Denver and Philadelphia)*

REVISIT THE BOOK

READER RESPONSE

1. Traveling traders call out to local traders; traveling traders leave their goods on the beach; local traders leave their goods on the beach; each group returns and decides if the trade is fair; different items are then added or removed to make trade fair.

2. The ancient Egyptians sent stones, copper, grains, and papyrus to ancient Lebanon. In return, they received wood such as fir, cedar, and pine.

3. Possible response: Sometimes two people who are bargaining have to compromise about a price.

4. Possible response: I could see the color and design of the coin.

EXTEND UNDERSTANDING Discuss with students how chapters in books can help organize complicated material. Go over the four chapters with students and discuss what information is in each chapter and why. Ask students how they can tell what each chapter is going to be about and how each chapter is a progression of the last.

RESPONSE OPTIONS

WRITING Have students imagine that for one day no money is available, so people must barter. Ask students to write a paragraph each about what that day would be like.

ELL Have students discuss whether bartering is common in their home country and, if so, whether it is used for certain types of goods and services or as a general practice.

SOCIAL STUDIES CONNECTION

Have students make up a new kind of money. Discuss whether their money will be coins or bills or something altogether different. Ask students how they will determine the value of their money and what it should look like. Once students have decided these things, ask them to make a grocery list showing what bread, milk, and fruit might cost with this new money.

Skill Work

TEACH/REVIEW VOCABULARY

Tell students you have chosen a word from the list of vocabulary words. It is their job to guess what the word is, based on clues you give. For example, "What word has three words in it?" (*bargaining, which has* bar, gain, *and* bargain *in it*)

TARGET SKILL AND STRATEGY

SEQUENCE Remind students that the *sequence* in a story is the order in which events occur. To illustrate, ask students to write a short paragraph about how to get from home to school, keeping the steps in sequence. Have students read their sequences to the class.

SUMMARIZE Remind students that *summarizing* means boiling down the main idea of a story or text into a sentence or two. In order to do this, students must identify the most important ideas or events. Ask students to summarize their last vacation or what they did over the weekend.

ADDITIONAL SKILL INSTRUCTION

DRAW CONCLUSIONS Remind students that *drawing conclusions* means to think about the facts and details that are presented and, sometimes with the benefit of personal experience, to decide something about them. By drawing conclusions, students can enhance their understanding of the text. Encourage students to draw conclusions as they read.

Sequence

- The **sequence** of events in a story is the order in which the events occur.

Directions Answer the questions on the lines below.

1. What is the sequence of events that goes on in bartering?

_____

_____

_____

2. What was the sequence of events in the trade between the Egyptians and the Lebanese?

_____

_____

_____

3. What happens during a silent trade? Summarize the steps.

_____

_____

_____

4. Trace the steps from bartering to the invention of coin money.

_____

_____

_____

5. Summarize why salt eventually was no longer used for money.

_____

_____

_____

Vocabulary

Directions Write the words from the box in the proper boxes. Note: There are three words that can go in both boxes. Use a dictionary to help you.

Check the Words You Know

___bargaining   ___compromise   ___currency
___mints   ___wampum

Nouns	Verbs

Directions Draw a line from the vocabulary word to its correct definition.

1. bargaining

2. compromise

3. currency

4. mints

5. wampum

a. to give up some of your demands to reach an agreement

b. money

c. beads made from shells

d. places where money is made

e. when two people work together to come up with an agreement

Journey Across the Arctic

SUMMARY Luca and Serena Cullen are a brother-and-sister adventure team who decide to do something no other brother and sister have done before: They want to trek across the Arctic to the North Pole in the deadly dark of winter. A sequence of events leads them to take their dangerous expedition to a remote part of the world.

LESSON VOCABULARY

efficient	lumbered
obstacle	renowned
rigorous	unstable

INTRODUCE THE BOOK

INTRODUCE THE TITLE AND AUTHOR Discuss with students the title and author of *Journey Across the Arctic*. Ask if students have traveled or taken part in sports in very cold weather. Ask what they remember about the weather. Explain that in this story, Luca and Serena have to contend with exteme weather.

BUILD BACKGROUND Display a map of Earth that shows the Arctic region. Ask students what they know about the North Pole. Explain that Luca and Serena's home was in Northern Europe, and locate Europe on the map. Point out Siberia, the Arctic Ocean, and frozen land between it and the North Pole.

PREVIEW/USE ILLUSTRATIONS Tell students that the genre of this book is fiction. Have students look through the illustrations. Discuss with students what they can tell about the boy and girl in the pictures and what they might be doing.

READ THE BOOK

SET PURPOSE Based on the genre and title of the book, have students tell why whey would like to read *Journey Across the Arctic*. Remind them that they may have more than one reason for wanting to read a book.

STRATEGY SUPPORT: VISUALIZE Tell students that *visualizing* is forming pictures in your mind about what is happening in the story. Explain to students that good readers visualize to make sense of the story or to enjoy it by placing themselves in the story. Tell students that as they read they will need to modify their original picture as they learn more information.

ELL Have students use a story sequence chart (see page 138) for *Journey Across the Arctic*. To check their understanding, have pairs of students exchange charts when they have finished reading.

COMPREHENSION QUESTIONS

PAGE 6 What are three things Luca would be responsible for in planning their future missions? *(raising money, determining supplies, arranging rescue squads)*

PAGE 9 What does it mean when Luca smiles and thinks that "his fate was sealed"? *(that he would indeed be taking a new adventure with Serena)*

PAGE 12 Why was it impossible for Luca and Serena to hike or ski straight up to the North Pole? *(The Arctic Ocean sometimes freezes all the way to shore, but other times it is unstable ice and open water.)*

PAGE 14 What were two things Luca was worried about when a severe storm hit? *(that their food supplies wouldn't last, and that spring would dawn before they reached the North Pole)*

PAGE 16 Why hadn't Serena told Luca that her ankle might be sprained? *(She was afraid that Luca would cancel the trip because she was in so much pain.)*

REVISIT THE BOOK

READER RESPONSE

1. Possible responses: chased away polar bear, had to cross icy water, storm hit, Serena sprained her ankle.
2. Responses will vary but should include details of page 12.
3. *Stable* must mean safe, solid, or secure; *unstable* means dangerous.
4. Possible response: I think there was just a little bit of light coming up in the sky, and it let them see all of the Arctic ice and snow they had crossed.

EXTEND UNDERSTANDING Point out to students that sometimes readers need to do a little research to make sense of what they will be reading. In *Journey Across the Arctic*, Luca and Serena must reach the North Pole before spring dawns. In other words, they must reach it before the months of total darkness end. This concept is challenging. Before students begin to read the book, direct them to the diagram on page 20 and its explanation of "Polar Night."

RESPONSE OPTIONS

WRITING Have students work in pairs to write about the next adventure Serena and Luca might take. Tell students to write the events they might encounter in sequence, so that there is a time order to what could happen.

SCIENCE CONNECTION

Have students research the Midnight Sun on the Internet or at the library. Direct students to write a report about their research and share their findings with the class.

Skill Work

TEACH/REVIEW VOCABULARY

Write a matching activity on the board with the vocabulary words in one column and definitions in another column. Direct students to the locations of the words in the book—*efficient*, page 4; *lumbered*, page 10; *obstacle*, page 5; *renowned*, page 3; *rigorous*, page 6; *unstable*, page 12. Then have them try to match each word to its correct definition using context clues.

TARGET SKILL AND STRATEGY

SEQUENCE Review with students that *sequence* is the order in which events occur. Remind them that, in a story, events are sometimes told out of their proper sequence. Sometimes the sequence of events may be interrupted to tell about events that happened earlier. Tell students to stop and reread parts of the story if they are not sure they are following the sequence of events correctly.

VISUALIZE After reading, encourage students to use their own experiences and knowledge to visualize the Arctic. Ask: Which details from the story helped you picture the Arctic? What knowledge or personal experiences helped you form your picture?

ADDITIONAL SKILL INSTRUCTION

SETTING Review with students that *setting* is the time and place in which events occur in a story. Have students point out the two main settings for this book—Serena and Luca's home and the Arctic itself. Invite students to guess when this story might have taken place. Tell them to look for clues to the time and place of the action in the story as they read.

Sequence

- **Sequence** is the order in which things happen in a story.

Directions Read the following passage. Then list the sequence of events that will lead to Serena and Luca's adventure across the Arctic in winter.

Ever since they were children, Serena and Luca dreamed of adventures. Together they hiked on snowshoes through the Alps; they skied along trails and to and from school.

When they were older, the siblings' first real expedition was a trek across the frozen ice fields of Patagonia in South America. For several years after that, the two traveled around the world to places few people had ever seen before.

One day, back at home, Serena was reading the newspaper when a headline caught her attention. The story told about two brothers who were planning to be the first sibling team to travel across the Arctic in winter. "But they are just *planning*," Serena said. "That means we could get there first!"

Luca knew his sister would pester him until he gave in to her dream. When she pointed out that she and Luca would be the first siblings to have a *woman* involved, he knew his fate was sealed. That night they began planning their most dangerous adventure yet.

First, _____

_____

Next, _____

_____

After that, _____

_____

Then, _____

_____

Finally, _____

_____

Vocabulary

Directions Choose the word from the box that best matches each definition. Write the word on the line.

Check the Words You Know
___efficient   ___lumbered   ___obstacle
___renowned   ___rigorous   ___unstable

1. _____ it prevents or stops something

2. _____ shaky; unsteady

3. _____ capable; competent

4. _____ famous; well-known

5. _____ moved along heavily and noisily

6. _____ severe; harsh

Directions Write a news article about Serena and Luca's trek across the Arctic in winter. Use as many of the vocabulary words as you can.

_____

_____

_____

_____

_____

_____

_____

_____

_____

_____

_____

The Road to New York

SUMMARY This realistic fiction story tells about a group of third-grade Double Dutch champions. They want to go to New York City to compete in the national championship, but they must earn a large sum of money to cover costs. The story supports the lesson focus of how we get what we want and need.

LESSON VOCABULARY

costly	donation
edit	obsessed
opportunity	promotional
sponsor	

INTRODUCE THE BOOK

INTRODUCE THE TITLE AND AUTHOR Discuss with students the title and author of *The Road to New York*. Direct them to look at the cover illustration to see if they can get a clue as to what the story might be about. Ask students to identify which elements in the illustration give them an idea of what they may be reading about.

BUILD BACKGROUND Ask students if they have ever been part of a winning team. Tell them that this book is about a Double Dutch jump rope team that wants to compete in New York, but that they must earn the money to get there. Discuss with students the different ways that third-graders might earn money.

PREVIEW/USE ILLUSTRATIONS As students preview the book, they may notice that the illustrations can tell a story on their own. Various illustrations show the champions jumping rope, worried team members, a serious older boy with camera, and finally a girl with pigtails and the older boy smiling. Explain that illustrations can give readers clues about what will take place in a story. Ask students to predict, based on the illustrations, what they think will happen in this story.

READ THE BOOK

SET PURPOSE Have students set a purpose for reading *The Road to New York*. Their interest in earning money or in Double Dutch should guide this purpose. Tell students that this story is also about a sister and brother who learn to get along better by working together on an important project.

STRATEGY SUPPORT: BACKGROUND KNOWLEDGE Review with students that *background knowledge* is what they already know about a topic. Encourage students to tell about competitions and fundraisers. Ask students what they may have learned about competitions and fundraisers. Explain that this background knowledge will help in understanding *The Road to New York*.

COMPREHENSION QUESTIONS

PAGES 4–5 How can you tell that the girl in pigtails, Julia, is an important member of the team? (*She holds the trophy on page 4; she is on a phone conversation with the Blazers' coach, Mr. Morse, on page 5, and she appears throughout the book.*)

PAGE 6 What do you think is Julia's opinion of her brother, Stuart? (*She thinks he is sarcastic and not very friendly to her.*)

PAGE 7 What did Stuart say that made Julia change her mind about giving up? (*that she needed to think like a Hollywood director*)

PAGE 14 What did Julia mean when she told Stuart "It's a job you'll like, and the pay is one hundred and fifty dollars"? (*that she and the Blazers wanted to hire him to make a pro-motional video*)

REVISIT THE BOOK

READER RESPONSE

1. Possible responses: Julia—works well in a team; Stuart—cares about filming movies by himself; Both—can work together for a common goal
2. Responses will vary but should include background knowledge and new information about Double Dutch.
3. improve
4. Possible response: Their relationship got better because they worked together to reach a goal.

EXTEND UNDERSTANDING As students read the story, remind them that students are able to work together to earn money for important projects such as the Blazers's trip to New York or, more realistically, for projects in the community. Ask for projects they might want to consider, and ask for ways they might earn money to help pay for one of the projects.

RESPONSE OPTIONS

WRITING Suggest that students consider why Stuart behaves as he does in the story. Ask them to imagine that they are Stuart. Have them write a letter from Stuart to Julia that tells why he acts the way he does.

SOCIAL STUDIES CONNECTION

Have students form small groups to research and report on the different aspects of the National Double Dutch League, such as the history, press releases, and events. Have each group make a presentation of the research to the class.

Skill Work

TEACH/REVIEW VOCABULARY

Reinforce the meanings of the vocabulary words by having students free-associate to come up with synonyms for the seven words.

ELL Suggest that students take a word, such as *costly*, and generate more words that mean the same thing. They can make a word web for each of the vocabulary words and follow this activity.

TARGET SKILL AND STRATEGY

COMPARE AND CONTRAST Remind students that to *compare and contrast* is to tell how things are alike and different. As students read, encourage them to compare and contrast characters, settings, and events in the story. Explain that making comparisons while they read can help them better understand the characters' motivations.

BACKGROUND KNOWLEDGE Share with students that *background knowledge* is what a reader already knows about a topic based on personal experience or reading. Invite students to look through the illustrations and ask how they remind them of their own lives. Suggest that students use background knowledge about competitions and fundraising to help them better understand the story and draw conclusions about what they have read.

ADDITIONAL SKILL INSTRUCTION

CHARACTER Remind students that *characters* are the people in a story who take part in the plot. Every character has traits, which are the things we know about the character that can help us predict how he or she will act in the story. Have students create a character chart for both Julia and Stuart. As they read, have students fill in the chart with traits of both characters.

Name _____

Compare and Contrast

- To **compare** is to tell how two or more things are alike.
- To **contrast** is to tell how two or more things are different.

Directions Use *The Road to New York* to compare and contrast raising money for a Double-Dutch competition with making a movie. Explain how they are similar and how they are different.

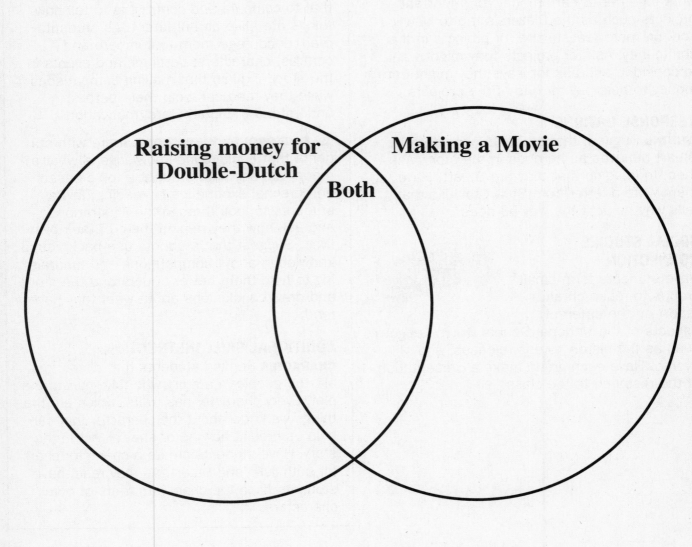

Vocabulary

Directions Write the correct vocabulary words in the blanks below.

> ### Check the Words You Know
> —costly   —donations   —edit   —obsessed
> —opportunity   —promotional   —sponsor

Julia and the Blazers had won their state's Double Dutch championship. Now they could go to New York and compete in the National Double Dutch Jump-Off. But with this wonderful **(1)** _____ came a big problem. It would be very **(2)** _____ to get to New York City. Mr. Morse made telephone calls to find a **(3)** _____ for the team's trip, but all he could come up with were small **(4)** _____. Julia's brother, Stuart, who was **(5)** _____ with making movies, teased her about not thinking like a Hollywood director. Stuart irritated his sister. But, after a bake sale and car wash earned only a few hundred dollars, Julia had an idea. She and her team would ask Stuart to make a **(6)** _____ video about the Blazers. After he shot the video, Stuart asked Julia to help him **(7)** _____ what he had filmed. In the end, the team earned the money—and Julia learned that Stuart wasn't such a bad brother after all.

8–10. Directions Select three vocabulary words and use each in a sentence.

_____

_____

_____

_____

3.1.5

⊚ **AUTHOR'S PURPOSE**
⊚ **STORY STRUCTURE**

With a Twist

SUMMARY This is a fantasy about how a group of children learns about different cultures when they magically travel around the world to buy ingredients for a popular meal—pizza. This story also shows how different people can have things in common.

LESSON VOCABULARY

awnings	bazaar
confused	garlic
ingredients	oregano
vendors	

INTRODUCE THE BOOK

INTRODUCE THE TITLE AND AUTHOR Discuss with students the title and the author of *With a Twist*. Based on the cover and the title, have students speculate what this book will be about.

BUILD BACKGROUND Discuss with students what it means to give something a "twist." Make sure students understand how the figurative meaning of *twist* is related to its literal meaning. Ask: What kinds of things can you twist literally (for real)? What kinds of things can you twist figuratively (in a manner of speaking)? Explain that many foods that we eat in the United States originated in other countries, and invite students to compare and contrast how their family's version of a common meal like pasta might differ from someone else's. How might different spices or ingredients add a "twist" to the meal?

PREVIEW/USE ILLUSTRATIONS Invite students to look at the illustrations and see if they can gain clues as to what this story might be about and where it might take place. Ask students what details help them with their answers.

READ THE BOOK

SET PURPOSE Have students set a purpose for reading *With a Twist*. Students' interest in pizza and their natural curiosity about what the "twist" in the story might be should guide this purpose. Suggest that students think about how changing, or "twisting," things can make them more interesting.

STRATEGY SUPPORT: STORY STRUCTURE As students read the story, suggest that they make notes about the sequence of events in the story. Ask them to consider whether any of the events could happen in any other order and how that might change the story.

COMPREHENSION QUESTIONS

PAGES 4, 12, 15 List some of the different settings of this book. *(Possible responses: a Russian street, a Greek market, Jake's house)*

PAGES 8–9 Do you think Bo, Ruby, and Jake have a good time on their journey through different cultures? Why do you think so? *(Possible response: Bo says he is really enjoying the trip; characters are smiling in the illustrations.)*

PAGE 15 Why do Bo, Ruby, and Jake cross items off their list? *(to make sure they have everything they need)*

PAGES 18–19 Write out the way Bo, Ruby, and Jake make pizza. Use the text structure of a recipe. *(Prepare pizza dough in the pan. Grate Parmesan cheese and slice mozzarella. For the sauce, chop tomatoes, basil, oregano, and garlic and cook them in a pan. Separately slice olives and pineapple. Spoon sauce over pizza dough, add the two cheeses, and arrange olives and pineapples on top. Place in oven and bake until done. Take out of oven, using mitts. Allow to cool slightly before cutting.)*

REVIST THE BOOK

READER RESPONSE

1. Possible response: to tell how foods we like have come from around the world
2. Peru—tomatoes; Italy—cheeses; India—basil; Russia—garlic; Greece—oregano and olives; Brazil—pineapple
3. *Unwrapped* means "removed the covering."
4. Possible response: I would visit Italy because I love Italian food.

EXTEND UNDERSTANDING Remind students that fantasy is an element in a story that isn't real. Discuss with students what elements of *With a Twist* are fantasy and why. Ask students how the addition of fantasy added to their enjoyment of the story and what information they learned through the fantasy that they wouldn't have learned otherwise.

RESPONSE OPTIONS

WRITING Suggest that students write about the places they would visit if they could snap their fingers the same way Jake does. Direct students to provide lots of sensory details to set their scenes.

SOCIAL STUDIES CONNECTION

Suggest that students think of their favorite food, such as pasta or Chinese noodles, and research the country where the food originated. Direct students to write a few sentences about their findings.

Skill Work

TEACH/REVIEW VOCABULARY

Review the vocabulary words. Discuss how the word *confused* has a suffix, *–ed,* that changes the meaning of the word. Ask students how the other vocabulary words can change their meanings by adding or removing suffixes and prefixes or by making them plural or singular.

ELL Have students write the definitions of the vocabulary words and use each word in a sentence.

TARGET SKILL AND STRATEGY

AUTHOR'S PURPOSE Tells students that an *author's purpose* is the reason an author writes a story, such as to inform, to entertain, to express, or to persuade. Ask students to discuss why they think an author might write about pizza. Ask: What do you think the author might like you to know?

STORY STRUCTURE Remind students that *story structure* is how a story is organized, with one event leading to another. To illustrate story structure, go through the book with the students and point out two events that are related. Then have students work in pairs to find other examples of related events.

ADDITIONAL SKILL INSTRUCTION

SEQUENCE Remind students that *sequence* is the order in which things happen. Suggest that as they read the story, students pay attention to how events happen. Give students a story outline in which the beginning, middle, and end are out of order, and invite them to restructure it.

Author's Purpose

- The **author's purpose** is the reason or reasons an author has for writing.
- An author may have one or more reasons for writing. He or she may want to **inform, persuade, entertain,** or **express** a mood or feeling.

Directions Read the passages and write the purpose you think the author had for writing each.

1. Jake snapped his fingers loudly, and suddenly everything was dark. The children felt like they were spinning through the air. After a few seconds it was light and they felt their feet back on the ground.

_____

2. The vendors were preparing to open the market. Children helped hang cloths from wooden frames around each stand. The vendors placed their goods on the tables in the stands.

_____

3. "I'm really enjoying this shopping trip," Bo said excitedly, as Jake snapped his fingers again. The children disappeared from the Italian food market.

_____

Directions Write a short paragraph about shopping at a grocery store. Choose one purpose for your paragraph. Write so that your purpose will be easily understood.

_____

_____

_____

_____

_____

Vocabulary

Directions Fill in the crossword puzzle by using the correct vocabulary word for each clue.

> ## Check the Words You Know
>
> ___awnings   ___bazaar   ___confused   ___garlic
> ___ingredients   ___oregano   ___vendors

ACROSS

2. a strong-smelling bulb used as seasoning
6. pieces of cloth stretched out to shade people from the sun
7. people who sell things in an open market

DOWN

1. parts that make up a recipe
3. not sure what is going on
4. a tasty herb used in pizza sauce and other Italian dishes
5. an open market in India

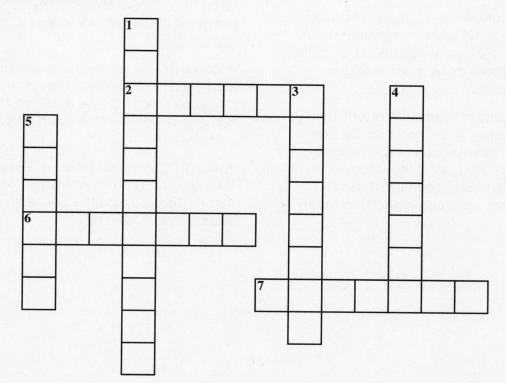

All About Penguins

SUMMARY Though Antarctica's emperor penguins are perhaps the best known birds of their kind, there are many other varieties of penguins that are just as interesting. The book describes how these birds are equipped to thrive in some of the coldest and most isolated places on Earth.

LESSON VOCABULARY

blubber	brood patch
crest	down
incubate	molt
rookery	

INTRODUCE THE BOOK

INTRODUCE THE TITLE AND AUTHOR Discuss with students the title and the author of *All About Penguins*. Ask them to look at the cover photo and describe what it tells about penguins. Based on their responses, talk about what information they think the author will provide in this book.

BUILD BACKGROUND Have students discuss what comes to mind when they think of penguins. Ask: How do penguins differ from other birds? Where do your ideas about penguins come from?

PREVIEW/USE TEXT FEATURES Point out the sidebars on pages 4, 5, 7, 9, and 13. Ask: What kinds of information can be found in these features? How does the information in each relate to the rest of the text, and why might the author have chosen to use them?

READ THE BOOK

SET PURPOSE Have students set a purpose for reading *All About Penguins*. They should be guided by their impressions from skimming the heads, photos, captions, and sidebars.

STRATEGY SUPPORT: MONITOR AND CLARIFY Tell students that they can *monitor* their comprehension of a story by creating an outline of it. An outline is a plan that shows how a story is organized. Using outlines to determine and keep track of the most important ideas of a book can help students gain comprehension. Invite students to create an outline of *All About Penguins* during and after reading. Have them *clarify* any questions they may have by referring them to their outlines.

COMPREHENSION QUESTIONS

PAGE 3 All penguins live in what part of the world? (*the Southern Hemisphere*)

PAGES 6–8 What is the topic of this section? What is the main idea of this section? (*emperor penguins; how they incubate their eggs*)

PAGE 11 How is an emperor penguin's beak shaped differently than that of an adelie penguin? (*Emperor's is long and thin to catch fish and Adelie's is short and stubby for catching krill.*)

PAGE 17 Different varieties of penguins share lives that are tied to what type of environment? (*the sea and the Southern Hemisphere's maritime ecosystems*)

REVIST THE BOOK

READER RESPONSE

1. Possible responses: Main idea: There are many different kinds of penguins in the world, and they all have ways to survive. Possible details: Their color protects them in the water; swimming fast means they can get away from their enemies; an emperor penguin has a brood patch to keep its egg warm; penguin feathers are oily so they shed water; penguins have blubber to give them energy and keep them warm; a rookery lets penguins protect each other; penguin eggs have hard shells.

2. Possible response: I wasn't sure if all penguins are alike, so I kept reading and learned about eleven different kinds of penguins—just half of all the kinds of penguins in the world.

3. Sentences will vary.

4. calcium; it thickens the penguins' eggshells.

EXTEND UNDERSTANDING Direct students to page 3. Ask: How does the map differ from most other maps you have seen? What continents are shown and where? Students may use a globe or atlas to help them find answers.

RESPONSE OPTIONS

WRITING Ask: How do people stay warm when they are outdoors in cold weather? How are these ways similar to or different from those of penguins? Have students answer these questions in one or two paragraphs.

WORD WORK Help students sort words related to aspects of penguins' lives into categories such as *body features, food,* and *dwellings.*

SCIENCE CONNECTION

Remind students that penguins have special characteristics that enable them to survive in specific types of environments. Have students research other animals in Antarctica, such as sea lions or orca whales, and find out what characteristics these animals have that make them suited to living there. Ask students to share their research.

Skill Work

TEACH/REVIEW VOCABULARY

Have students look at the Glossary. Ask volunteers to point out familiar terms and explain what they mean.

ELL On the board, write simple sentences that students can complete by writing a vocabulary word or two, for example: *Penguins have a layer of _____ that stores energy and blocks out cold.*

TARGET SKILL AND STRATEGY

MAIN IDEA AND DETAILS The *main idea* is the most important idea about the topic. To find it, students must determine the relative importance of information they read. *Supporting details* are pieces of information that tell more about the main idea. Model how to ask questions to find the main idea of a book. Ask: In a word or two, what is this book about? (This identifies the topic.) What is the most important idea about the topic? (This identifies the main idea.) What are some details that tell more about the main idea? Tell students to identify the main idea of the book as they read.

MONITOR AND CLARIFY Remind students that good readers often *monitor* their comprehension, or ask themselves if they understand what they are reading. If something seems confusing or does not make sense, good readers take steps to figure out the problem. Reading on, rereading, or asking a partner or an expert are ways to *clarify* confusing points.

ADDITIONAL SKILL INSTRUCTION

COMPARE AND CONTRAST Tell students that to *compare* is to identify how two or more things are alike and to *contrast* is to identify how they are different. Ask students to use graphic organizers to compare and contrast aspects of different penguins in the book, such as their natural habitats.

Name _____

Main Idea and Details

- The **main idea** is the most important idea about a paragraph, passage, or story.
- **Supporting details** are pieces of information that tell more about the main idea.

Directions Read each passage. Then answer the questions that follow.

> The Southern Hemisphere is the natural home to the world's penguins. Penguins live on the Galápagos Islands and in Australia, New Zealand, Africa, South America, and the islands that surround Antarctica. They also live on Antarctica itself. All penguins share lives that are tied to the sea and the Southern Hemisphere's marine ecosystems.

1. In a few words, what is this paragraph about?

_____

2. What is the main idea of the paragraph?

_____

3. What is an important detail that tells more about the main idea?

_____

_____

> Emperor penguins reduce heat loss through their feet by standing on their heels. This keeps the rest of the foot from touching cold ice.
>
> Male emperor penguins also huddle to help conserve heat. The temperature in the middle of an emperor penguin huddle can be 95°F! Of course, some penguins must stand on the outside of the huddle. So what do they do to stay warm? They rotate. The penguins on the outside gradually push their way into the middle of the huddle. This way, each penguin gets a chance to become warmed.

4. What is the main idea of the passage?

_____

_____

5. What is one detail that tells more about the main idea?

_____

_____

Vocabulary

Directions Choose the word from the box that best completes each sentence. Write the word on the line.

Check the Words You Know
___blubber ___brood patch ___crest ___down
___incubate ___molt ___rookery

1. Emperor penguins choose to _____ their eggs during the winter.

2. Large groups of penguins gather in a _____ to raise their young.

3. A penguin's _____ stores energy and helps protect the penguin from cold weather.

4. Fluffy inner feathers known as _____ trap air to keep penguins warm.

5. Penguins _____ when their old feathers get worn out.

6. Male penguins have a featherless area of skin known as a

   _____, which warms their eggs.

7. Some penguins have a _____ that sticks up from their heads.

Directions Use the context clues in the above sentences to define these words.

8. molt _____

_____

9. rookery _____

_____

10. blubber _____

_____

Puppy Problems

SUMMARY Zoë has moved away from her best friend, Lila, because of her mom's new job as governor. She e-mails Lila about her excitement at finally getting a dog of her own. But when Zoë learns she is allergic to most dogs, she is told she may need to buy a purebred dog rather than one from a shelter. Public opinion goes against her, but Lila saves the day by finding a purebred, non-allergenic miniature schnauzer on a shelter's Web site. Zoë gets her pound puppy after all.

LESSON VOCABULARY

abandoned	allergic
apologizing	attachment
conference	embarrassing
rally	union

INTRODUCE THE BOOK

INTRODUCE THE TITLE AND AUTHOR Discuss with students the title and the author of *Puppy Problems*. Ask: What kinds of problems might people have with choosing a puppy? Ask them to think beyond the adorable qualities for which puppies are known.

BUILD BACKGROUND Ask students if they have ever known someone who was allergic to animals. Explain that many people are allergic to cats and that some people are allergic to dogs as well. People who decide they want a dog (or a cat) despite allergies need to choose a breed that has few if any allergens. Because shelters have mostly mixed-breed dogs (and cats), people with allergies usually have to buy purebred animals from a breeder.

PREVIEW/USE ILLUSTRATIONS Have students skim through the book, looking at the pictures. Ask: What do you think the story is about? Who are the characters? How do they communicate, and where does the story appear to take place? Can you tell that there may be an underlying story about the characters as well as the story about a puppy?

READ THE BOOK

SET PURPOSE Have students set a purpose for reading *Puppy Problems*. This purpose should be guided by the impressions they get from reading the title and skimming the illustrations along with their own curiosity.

STRATEGY SUPPORT: VISUALIZE Remind students how to *visualize*. To visualize means that as you read, you form pictures in your mind about what is happening in the story. Tell students that they should combine what they already know with details from the text to create pictures in their mind. Add that they can use all of their senses, not just sight, to help them form pictures.

COMPREHENSION QUESTIONS

PAGES 3–4 What can you tell about Zoë and Lila from their e-mails? *(They are good friends who want to stay in close touch with one another.)*

PAGE 12 What does the newspaper headline tell you about public opinion regarding adopting from a shelter? *(Many people think it's a good and compassionate idea.)*

PAGES 13–14 What prompted Zoë to talk about her puppy problem with the reporters? *(She was frustrated that her mom and dad weren't around to talk with about the need to choose a special breed of non-allergenic dog.)*

PAGE 17 Why do you think public opinion about the puppy adoption changed into a protest rally against Zoë? *(People who had supported her shelter adoption now thought of her as a spoiled kid who would be happy only with a high-priced dog.)*

PAGE 19 Why did purebred dog breeders threaten to boycott every pet food company that had donated money to the new governor's election? *(They believed that the new governor and her family had taken a stand against purebred dogs and wanted to get attention on their own behalf.)*

REVISIT THE BOOK
READER RESPONSE

1. Adopt: Many stray and abandoned dogs need a home; many people say mutts make the best pets. Buy: Purebred dogs usually have predictable behavior and looks; some people just prefer a specific breed. Both: Adopting or buying a dog means that the dog will go to someone's home and have a chance at a happy life.

2. Responses will vary but should indicate that Zoë was in great discomfort at the shelter.

3. Responses will vary but need to reflect correct use of three of the vocabulary words.

4. The reporters had praised Zoë's wish to adopt a shelter puppy and may have felt betrayed—or confused—by her worrying about needing to choose a purebred dog. Responses to the second question will vary.

EXTEND UNDERSTANDING Explore the element of *plot* with students by asking questions such as "What does the author want readers to learn from reading this story?" Explain that there are several plots in *Puppy Problems*: Zoë and Lila's friendship remains strong even though they no longer live close together; Zoë's wish to adopt a dog—one she's not allergic to; the ability of a young girl to make the news because of her mom's new, public role as governor. Ask students if they remember a First Family that had to forgo adopting a pound puppy because of allergies.

RESPONSE OPTIONS

WRITING Ask students to write an e-mail to Zoë about her choices, with advice on how she may need to be careful of what she says in the future.

SOCIAL STUDIES CONNECTION

Provide appropriate nonfiction books about purebred dogs and their roles with humans, and invite students to use the Internet to learn more about both purebred dogs and the mixed-breed dogs that are typically found in shelters for homeless animals. Have them share what they learn with the class.

Skill Work

TEACH/REVIEW VOCABULARY

Read the vocabulary words. Ask students about words they may already know. Discuss how they first heard of the words and what they think the words mean. Tell them that they will become more familiar with these words as they read.

ELL Have students write the translation for each vocabulary word in their home languages and then write the English word beside it. Listen for cognates they find.

TARGET SKILL AND STRATEGY

COMPARE AND CONTRAST Remind students that to *compare* two or more things, they describe how those things are alike. To *contrast* is to describe only how the things are different. Have students tell what a shelter dog may be like (*a dog to love, usually a mixed-breed that is a surprise in personality and looks*). Next compare that to a purebred dog (*also a dog to love but that is predictable in personality and looks*). Then have them contrast the two types of pets.

VISUALIZE Tell students that to visualize is to form a picture in their minds about what is happening in the story. Encourage students to try to visualize the behind-the-scenes events and characters in *Puppy Problems* as they read it. Ask them to describe what they think Zoë's mom must have looked like when she heard that her daughter now wanted a purebred dog.

ADDITIONAL SKILL INSTRUCTION

CAUSE AND EFFECT Remind students that an effect is something that happens and a cause is why that thing happens. Have students practice identifying cause and effect in simple sentences such as "The reporters wrote negatively about Zoë because she now said she would get a purebred dog." (What happened: the reporters wrote negatively about Zoë. Why it happened: she changed from wanting to adopt a shelter dog to needing to buy a purebred.)

Compare and Contrast

- When you **compare** two or more things, you think about how they are alike and how they are different.
- When you **contrast** two or more things, you only think about how they are different.

Directions Look back at *Puppy Problems* to complete the chart. Fill in the chart with information based on what you learned from the book and from your Internet research on pound puppies and purebred dogs.

Pound Puppy	Purebred Dog
1. _____ _____	3. _____ _____
2. _____ _____	4. _____ _____

5. Write a paragraph that compares and contrasts a pound puppy to a purebred dog. Use the chart, the story, and your own experience as you write.

_____

_____

_____

_____

_____

Name _____

Vocabulary

Directions Write the word from the box that best completes each sentence.

Check the Words You Know

___abandoned ___allergic ___apologizing ___attachment
___conference ___embarrassing ___rally ___union

1. Zoë wanted to find a puppy that had been _____ or was a stray.

2. The new governor met with members of the teachers' _____

3. Lila's e-mail included an _____ about a purebred miniature schnauzer.

4. The puppy problem started when Zoë learned she was _____ to most dogs.

5. Zoë's mom had to call a press _____ about the choice of a new dog.

6. The governor found herself _____ to breeders of purebred dogs.

7. Zoë probably found her new situation as first daughter both

   _____ and a little scary.

8. People may get together for a _____ for any of many reasons.

Directions What do you think happened to Zoë and her family and the new dog after the story ended? Write a paragraph about what you think their lives might be like. Use as many vocabulary words as you can.

_____

_____

_____

_____

_____

A Family of Collectors

SUMMARY Tina cannot understand why her mother loves collecting teacups. Tina later discovers the joy of collecting while searching for a birthday gift for her mother and sees her mother's teacups in a whole new light.

LESSON VOCABULARY

collectibles	credit
fond	kaleidoscope
porcelain	propped
rim	specialize
suspiciously	

INTRODUCE THE BOOK

INTRODUCE THE TITLE AND AUTHOR Discuss with students the title and the author of *A Family of Collectors*. Ask: Based on the title, do you think the story will be fiction or nonfiction? Why? Then have them look at the cover illustration and talk about how the title might relate to the picture.

BUILD BACKGROUND Ask students if they collect objects such as dolls or baseball cards. What makes those objects so special? Discuss reasons why people collect things in general.

PREVIEW/USE TEXT FEATURES Have students preview the book by looking at the title and illustrations. What predictions can they make about the story based on these features?

READ THE BOOK

SET PURPOSE Have students set a purpose for reading *A Family of Collectors*. Students' own interest in collecting objects should guide this purpose. Suggest that they think about what collections can reveal about the interests and personalities of collectors.

STRATEGY SUPPORT: QUESTIONING Remind students that asking key questions before they read a story can help keep them focused. Asking questions during and after reading, and answering the questions they have raised, helps comprehension by getting the reader more involved in what he or she is reading.

ELL Use a graphic organizer to show steps in a process. Help students outline the steps that Tina and her father took to find a gift for Tina's mother.

COMPREHENSION QUESTIONS

PAGE 6 Early in the book, how did Tina feel about her mother's collection of teacups? *(Tina pretended to like teacups but did not understand her mother's fascination with them.)*

PAGE 8 How did Tina's father feel about his wife's teacups? *(He supported her hobby as seen in the trip to the collectibles fair.)*

PAGE 23 How did Tina's feelings about her mother's teacups change by the end of the book? *(When Tina bought a collectible kaleidoscope at the fair, she understood why her mother loved collecting pretty objects.)*

REVISIT THE BOOK

READER RESPONSE

1. Responses should indicate that Tina has grown to respect her mother's collection and to become interested in collecting as well.
2. Responses will vary but should show a connection to the story and the idea of making a collection. The answer to the second question should relate to the question(s) the student raised about collections.
3. Possible responses: Fact 1—a tube of mirrors containing loose–colored beads. Fact 2—the name was coined in 1817 by its inventor Sir David Brewster. Fact 3—the part which holds objects to be viewed is called an object chamber. Fact 4—operate on the principle of multiple reflection where several mirrors are attached together.
4. Possible response: Buy the kaleidoscope sooner.

EXTEND UNDERSTANDING Tell students that a *character* is someone who takes part in the events of a story. *Character traits* are the qualities of a character and are often related to personality. Select a c haracter from the book and invite students to identify his or her traits. Students must tell what elements of the story suggest that the character possesses these traits.

RESPONSE OPTIONS

WRITING Remind students that Tina's father brought along photos of his wife's teacups and memorized details about her preferences while shopping for her gift. Invite students to write about a time when they faced a similar challenge (gift-related or not) and what strategies they used to tackle it.

WORD WORK Play a game that will challenge students to identify the correct meanings of vocabulary words. Write the proper definition of each word on a separate index card while providing students with cards where they can write made-up definitions for the vocabulary (the sillier the better). Then read aloud each word along with the correct and made-up definitions for it and have students vote on the proper meaning.

Skill Work

TEACH/REVIEW VOCABULARY
Have volunteers show how the vocabulary words are used in the book. Then ask them how each word helped them better understand the story and its characters.

TARGET SKILL AND STRATEGY
DRAW CONCLUSIONS Remind students that to *draw conclusions* about a story means to decide what it means after thinking about facts and details. Have students ask the following questions as they read: Why do some people begin to make a collection of something? What does a collector gain from his or her collection?

QUESTIONING Tell students that *questioning* is a good way to tap into their curiosity as they read something. Questions can anticipate what a story will be about or why the author wrote it, locate or find new information, and guide the reader to do independent research about the topic of the story. Encourage students to ask themselves relevant questions and to answer them fully as they read.

ADDITIONAL SKILL INSTRUCTION
REALISM AND FANTASY Explain that a *realistic story* tells about something that could happen, and a *fantasy* is a story about something that could not happen. Tell students that while they are reading they should identify specific events within *A Family of Collectors* that indicate the type of story it is. Invite them to discuss how the author could change the book to make it the other type of story.

SOCIAL STUDIES CONNECTION
Divide students into groups and have each group choose a type of antique toy to research. Invite students to create a fact sheet about the toy and share their information with the class.

Draw Conclusions

- To draw a conclusion is to think about facts and details and decide something that makes sense about them.

Directions Read the following passage from *A Family of Collectors*. Then write two facts and draw a conclusion.

> Dad was right. The next place had very good prices. We found a pretty cup and saucer that were both in good shape, and they were decorated with gold rims. But when Dad turned the cup over he shook his head.
>
> "It's made in France, not England," he said. "And I think this pattern is very similar to one your mom already has." He checked the photos, pulled one out, and pointed. "See? It's almost the same."

1. Fact:

_____

2. Fact:

_____

3. Conclusion:

_____

Directions Read the following passage. Then write two facts on the lines below. See what conclusion you can draw from them about Tina's attitude toward collecting.

> Tina held her kaleidoscope up to the light and looked inside. She felt a dreamy smile spreading across her face, a smile just like the ones on her mom's face when she looks at her teacups!

4–5. Facts:

_____

_____

6. Conclusion:

_____

Vocabulary

Directions Choose the word from the box that best completes each sentence. Write the word on the line.

Check the Words You Know

___collectibles   ___credit   ___fond
___kaleidoscope   ___porcelain   ___propped
___rim   ___specialize   ___suspiciously

---

1. The spoon was resting on the _____ of the teacup.

2. Tina worked hard to find the perfect present, so she deserves

   the _____ for finding such a nice gift.

3. You can see beautiful colors and patterns if you look through

   a _____.

4. An antiques market is a great place for buyers to find _____.

5. The teacher looked at the boy _____ when he tried
   to hide candy in his desk.

6. She was especially _____ of long walks on warm
   summer nights.

7. Please handle the _____ dishes carefully, because they
   break easily.

8. The broom is _____ against the closet door.

9. I brought my broken antique doll to people who_____
   in repairing toys.

The Magic of Coyote

SUMMARY This is a story about the cost of being afraid and the benefit of overcoming your fear. With the help of a Navaho storyteller and a dog that is part coyote, a boy learns to conquer his fear of dogs. This story also introduces the concept of *fable,* a story with talking animals that teaches a lesson.

LESSON VOCABULARY

artifacts	breakthrough
cunning	descendant
retreated	scampered
yelping	

INTRODUCE THE BOOK

INTRODUCE THE TITLE AND AUTHOR Discuss with students the title and the author of *The Magic of Coyote.* Based on the title, ask students what they imagine this book might be about and whether the title indicates that the book is fiction or nonfiction. Note the word *magic* in the title, and discuss what it might indicate.

BUILD BACKGROUND Within this story, a Navajo storyteller shares a traditional Navajo tale about a clever coyote who teaches humans to use fire. Discuss with students other fictional tales they've encountered in which animals are smart and can talk or behave like people.

PREVIEW/USE TEXT FEATURES As students preview the book, draw their attention to the clouds pictured above the main character's head on pages 4 and 17. Ask students what these clouds mean and why they think the artist drew them. Discuss how *thought balloons* add to the story.

READ THE BOOK

SET PURPOSE Have students set a purpose for reading *The Magic of Coyote.* Students' interest in conquering their fears of dogs (or something else) should guide this purpose. Suggest that students think about the cost of being afraid and the benefits of facing their fears.

STRATEGY SUPPORT: PREDICT As students read about Henry grappling with his fear of dogs, predicting what may happen next in the story can give students a chance to reinforce what they already know. Making predictions also deepens students' involvement in the story and gives them a stake in the story's outcome.

COMPREHENSION QUESTIONS

PAGE 3 What details show you why Henry is afraid of dogs? *(They yelp and have sharp teeth and unpleasant smells.)*

PAGE 10 What clues show that Mr. Gordon's story is fiction? *(Coyote understands human conversation; coyote feels sympathy; fire beings don't really exist.)*

PAGE 21 Ranger is part coyote and part dog. Why does this help soothe Henry's fears? *(He already likes coyotes from the story. He is only afraid of the "dog" part of Ranger.)*

PAGES 21–22 What do you think the author's purpose was in having Henry pet Ranger? *(The author wanted to show that when Henry faced his fear and touched the dog, he started to get over his fear.)*

REVISIT THE BOOK

READER RESPONSE

1. Possible response: to give information about Navajo culture and to show how a story can help you get over your fears
2. Possible response: Henry will probably be much less scared around dogs. The more he is around dogs, the less frightened he will be.
3. brunch=breakfast, lunch; motel=motor, hotel; moped=motor, pedal; paratroops=parachute, troops; skylab=sky, laboratory; smog=smoke, fog: telethon=telephone, marathon
4. Responses will vary.

EXTEND UNDERSTANDING Tell students that stories that involve talking animals are common worldwide, from Aesop's fables to Navajo coyote tales to C.S. Lewis's *Chronicles of Narnia.* Encourage students to discuss what it is about animals that makes them useful as characters in stories that teach a lesson, explain an idea, or show us something about ourselves.

RESPONSE OPTIONS

WORD WORK Play a true or false word game with students. Using the vocabulary words, put the words in sentences and ask students if the words have been used correctly. For example: After the student read twenty books, she *retreated* into her room to watch TV. Do the same with all of the vocabulary words. Encourage students to write their own "true or false" sentences using the vocabulary words in this lesson.

SOCIAL STUDIES CONNECTION

Time For SOCIAL STUDIES

Invite students to learn more about the lives of Navajo children. Encourage them to use research books or the Internet. Ask them to write them short reports on what they find and to present them to the class.

Skill Work

TEACH/REVIEW VOCABULARY

Write the vocabulary words on the board. Have volunteers look up their definitions and share them with the class. Invite discussion as to how each word contributes to a story. For example, if a character is described as *cunning*, what might you expect from the character?

ELL Word studies can often make vocabulary more memorable. Demonstrate how *breakthrough* divides into *break* and *through*. Discuss the meanings of the separate words and then what they mean together. Show that *descendant* is related to *descend,* which means "to come down." Use a diagram with *grandparents* on top, then *parents,* then *children,* to show how *descend* means going down. Review that *-ed* at the end of several words makes them past tense.

TARGET SKILL AND STRATEGY

AUTHOR'S PURPOSE Remind students that the *author's purpose* is the reason why the author wrote the story. An author might want to entertain, inform, express, or persuade. Have them look for clues and details that reveal why the author might have written the story.

PREDICT Remind students that to *predict* means to guess what will happen next in a story based on what has happened before. As students read, suggest that they predict what will make Henry less afraid of dogs. Ask students to write their predictions. After they've read the story, have them review their predictions to see which ones were right.

ADDITIONAL SKILL INSTRUCTION

SEQUENCE Remind students that the *sequence of events* is the order in which events happen in a story. Have students do a story map of the book, placing major events under the headings "beginning of the story," "middle of the story," and "end of the story." As students read, ask them to write down any clue words or phrases that might help them with sequence, such as *after* or *the next day.*

Author's Purpose

- The **author's purpose** is the reason or reasons the author has for writing.
- An author may have one or more reasons for writing. Common reasons are to *inform, persuade, entertain,* or *express.*

Directions Answer the questions.

1. What do you think is the author's purpose for writing this story?

_____

_____

_____

2. What do you think is the author's purpose for including the story about Coyote?

_____

_____

_____

3. How does the story about Coyote stealing fire help Henry?

_____

_____

_____

4. What do you think the author wants you to learn about Navajo culture?

_____

_____

_____

5. Why do you think the author had Henry meet a coydog?

_____

_____

_____

Vocabulary

Directions Complete each sentence in the story with one of the vocabulary words.

> ### Check the Words You Know
> ___artifacts   ___breakthrough   ___cunning   ___descendant
> ___retreated   ___scampered   ___yelping

Henry was afraid of the (**1**) _____ dogs. Every time he saw

them, he (**2**) _____ to the back of the room.

One day, Henry and his class visited a Native American museum. First they

studied ancient (**3**) _____, such as pieces of pottery. Then it was time

for a story.

The story was told by Mr. Gordon, who was a (**4**) _____ of a

Navajo storyteller. Mr. Gordon told tales about the coyote, a (**5**) _____

creature who often played tricks on the Navajo people. Henry discovered that his

interest in coyotes made him feel less afraid about dogs. When Mr. Gordon's coydog,

Ranger, (**6**) _____ over to Henry, Henry actually petted Ranger. Henry

was excited, because he knew this was a real (**7**) _____.

Directions Write the definition of each word based on its context above.
Use a dictionary if necessary.

8. retreated _____

_____

9. breakthrough _____

_____

10. yelping _____

_____

Animals of the Concrete Jungle

SUMMARY This book presents unexpected animals that are now making their homes in cities—raptors, alligators, bats, and even tropical parrots in Brooklyn, New York. It explains how and why these animals have located to urban areas and gives readers a good connection to the week's focus of how plants and animals have adapted to solve problems.

LESSON VOCABULARY

abundance	emerge
loom	populous
raptors	thriving
traipsing	vivid

INTRODUCE THE BOOK

INTRODUCE THE TITLE AND AUTHOR Discuss with students the title and the author of *Animals of the Concrete Jungle*. Ask them to describe animals they have seen in cities—perhaps squirrels, pigeons and other birds, raccoons, even rats. Have them look at the cover and predict the kinds of animals this book may be about.

BUILD BACKGROUND Tell students that animals that once lived only in wild areas sometimes move into cities and suburbs. Invite them to think about why this might happen. For example, rural and wild areas are being turned into housing developments and shopping centers, which may leave animals without places to live.

PREVIEW/USE TEXT FEATURES Ask students to leaf through the pages and look at the photos. Based on these images, what can they tell about the kinds of animals that will be discussed in this book? What do the photos that appear at the bottom of most pages suggest about the setting for this book?

READ THE BOOK

SET PURPOSE Have students set a purpose for reading *Animals of the Concrete Jungle*. Their knowledge of animals usually found in urban areas and those that would seem foreign to cities should guide this purpose. Suggest that students think about how the animals pictured reflect different parts of the United States.

STRATEGY SUPPORT: ASK QUESTIONS Explain that *text structure* is the organizational pattern in which a selection is put together. *Animals of the Concrete Jungle*, an example of expository nonfiction, both tells a story and informs. Its structure includes photos and captions to make information easy to find and read.

COMPREHENSION QUESTIONS

PAGE 3 Why are cities sometimes called "concrete jungles"? (*because they have so much concrete in sidewalks and streets*)

PAGE 5 Name two kinds of birds that are known as raptors. (*hawks and falcons*)

PAGE 8 What is one reason the people of Austin, Texas, might hold a festival each August for their Mexican free-tailed bats? (*the bats eat so many mosquitoes*)

PAGE 11 The wealth of food in a city lures which three kinds of wild animals? (*deer, bears, raccoons*)

PAGE 16 What is the ratio of alligators to humans in Florida? (*1 alligator to every 18 humans*)

REVISIT THE BOOK

READER RESPONSE

1. The main idea is that animals are living inside cities, often far from their native habitats. Details: Mexican free-tailed bats live in the middle of downtown Austin, Texas; raptors have settled into big cities with tall buildings; monk parakeets live in places like Brooklyn, New York.
2. Possible response: The first sentence states that coyotes are suited to city life, so I knew that the paragraph would be about coyotes that live in cities.
3. Sentences will vary but must use three vocabulary words correctly.
4. Responses will vary depending on where students live.

EXTEND UNDERSTANDING Ask students to carefully study the close-up photos of Pale Male on the cover and of his nest on pages 4–5. Discuss what students know about hawks that suggests why Pale Male might be shown near a skyscraper and why he built his nest on a twelfth-floor ledge.

RESPONSE OPTIONS

WRITING Ask students to write a letter to someone who lives in a rural area telling that person about the animals that have been spotted living in cities. Have students explain how each animal has adapted to its urban habitat.

ELL Have students draw a picture of an urban animal they may have seen when they visited or lived in another country.

SCIENCE CONNECTION

Tell students that scientists study ways that wild animals adapt to new urban habitats. Direct them to pages 12–13, which tell about the decline and recovery of the cougar, or mountain lion, population. Ask what other species of animals seem suited to survival in cities.

Skill Work

TEACH/REVIEW VOCABULARY

Have students create bookmarks on which they can list new words they discover while reading. On the bookmarks they may write their names, the book title, the new words, and the page numbers on which the words appeared. After reading, ask students to share their words with the class.

TARGET SKILL AND STRATEGY

MAIN IDEA AND DETAILS Remind students that *main idea* is the most important idea about a story, paragraph, or passage. It is the answer to the question "What is it all about?" Details that support the main idea tell the reader more about that idea. Model: *Animals of the Concrete Jungle* is all about animals that are living inside cities, often far from their native habitats. What are some of the details that back up this main idea?

TEXT STRUCTURE The author of *Animals of the Concrete Jungle* has organized the text by groups of animals. Animals that fly are written about first. Then the author writes about animals that live on land. Finally, she writes about alligators, which as amphibians live on both land and in the water. Recognizing the structure of a text is another way to aid comprehension.

ADDITIONAL SKILL INSTRUCTION

FACT AND OPINION A statement of *fact* can be proved true or false by consulting reference books and using other evidence. An *opinion* is a judgment or belief that cannot be proven true or false. Tell students that nonfiction books such as *Animals of the Concrete Jungle* are likely to contain statements of fact. Invite students to identify a fact from the book and a reference source for verifying that fact. Then ask them to make statements of opinion about the book.

Main Idea and Details

- The **main idea** is the most important idea about a paragraph, passage, or story.
- **Details** are pieces of information that tell more about the main idea.

Directions Read the following passage. Then answer the questions below.

In the mid-1950s, the American alligator was nearly extinct due to hunting. In 1962, Florida passed a law that banned the hunting of American alligators. In 1970, a much stronger federal law made it a federal offense to ship illegally hunted alligators across state lines.

As a result, the population of these reptiles has increased over the years. Today, alligators are a common sight throughout Florida. They've even turned up at popular amusement parks! More than one million alligators now live in Florida, where more than 18 million people live.

1. Use one sentence to tell what this passage is about.

_____

2. What is the main idea of the passage?

_____

3–4. What are two details that tell more about the main idea?

_____

_____

5–7. Imagine you are telling people about the book *Animals of the Concrete Jungle.* Write below the main idea of what you would tell them and then add two details to support the main idea.

Main Idea:

_____

Details:

_____

_____

Vocabulary

Directions Write the word from the box that matches each definition below.

Check the Words You Know

___abundance   ___emerge   ___loom   ___populous
___raptors   ___thriving   ___traipsing   ___vivid

1. _____ strikingly bright; brilliant

2. _____ much more than enough

3. _____ growing rich or strong

4. _____ full of people or animals

5. _____ appear as a threatening shape

6. _____ walking about aimlessly or carelessly

7. _____ to come into view or come out

8. _____ birds that live by hunting small animals

9–10. Directions Write two sentences about urban animals from the book. Use as many vocabulary words as you can.

_____

_____

_____

_____

_____

_____

_____

Grape Season

SUMMARY This fictional story about a migrant worker family includes some facts about migrant workers in California.

LESSON VOCABULARY

campsite	crop
elevation	migrant workers
sequoias	snowcapped
trailhead	trunk

INTRODUCE THE BOOK

INTRODUCE THE TITLE AND AUTHOR Discuss the title and author of *Grape Season*. Invite students to speculate about the connection between the title and the illustration.

BUILD BACKGROUND Explain to students that some families work in the fields in California and elsewhere. The families, called migrant workers, must move around to pick crops as they become ripe.

PREVIEW/USE TEXT FEATURES Have students preview the book by paging through it and looking at the illustrations. Ask: What do you think you will read about in this book? What makes you think so? What makes you think that page 21 is nonfiction?

READ THE BOOK

SET PURPOSE Recall with students that they should use what they learned as they previewed the book to help them set a purpose for reading. Remind them that their purpose might change as they read and find out what the book is really about.

STRATEGY SUPPORT: IMPORTANT IDEAS Remind students that good readers recognize which ideas they read are the most important. Explain that as students read they should try to identify the most important ideas. Model questions to ask while reading such as: Is this idea important? Or is it a small detail?

COMPREHENSION QUESTIONS

PAGE 3 How does Miguel's family earn money? *(They pick grapes in the fields where they grow.)*

PAGES 7–10 What wonderful surprise did Tío Hector have for Miguel and his sister? *(He wanted to take them on a camping vacation to Sequoia National Park.)* Why was Miguel so very thrilled? *(He had never had a vacation, especially one like this that he could brag about to the other kids in school.)*

PAGES 16–17 What is unusual about sequoia trees? *(They are huge. One, the General Sherman tree, is the world's largest tree, and it is more than 2,300 years old.)*

PAGE 20 What lesson did Miguel learn on the trip? *(He figured out that nature brought more to life than work.)*

ELL Make sure all students understand the Spanish words and phrases used in the book. Enlist the help of students who speak Spanish to explain the meanings of *Tía* (aunt), *Tío* (uncle), and *mi hijo* (my son) and to provide pronunciations.

REVISIT THE BOOK

READER RESPONSE

1. Responses may vary, but most students will conclude that Miguel's family feels that their hard work is very important to them. Some clues students may find include that the children work hard even before they are old enough to go into the fields, their parents have never taken a vacation, and their father is afraid that if the children go with Tío Hector, they will not get their work done.

2. Ideas and their relative importance will vary. Some possibilities include: 1. Miguel learned that nature brought more to life than work. 2. Migrant workers, including their children, work extremely hard. 3. Miguel envied the children in his school who always went on summer vacation. 4. When camping, it is necessary to keep food in metal boxes to keep it protected from bears.

3. On page 11, *trunk* means the storage area at the back of a car. On page 16, the word means the central stem of a tree. Discuss with students the context clues that helped them figure out the two meanings.

4. Responses will vary. Invite students to compare their ideas of a camping trip to Miguel's camping experience.

EXTEND UNDERSTANDING Tell students that historically, migrant workers have often been exploited by their employers because they were paid very little and had to work in extremely difficult conditions. In the mid-1960s, a man named César Chávez formed a union of migrant workers who worked in the California grape fields. The workers went on strike and refused to work until their working conditions were improved. They eventually won, and the owners had to improve the working conditions.

RESPONSE OPTIONS

ART Invite students to illustrate their own favorite campsite. Point out that their favorite does not have to be real or a place they have actually been.

DRAMA CONNECTION

Suggest that students put on a play based on the book *Grape Season*. Have teams work on different aspects of the production: writing, acting, props, and so on. Encourage them to put on the play for another class, perhaps of younger students.

Skill Work

TEACH/REVIEW VOCABULARY

Provide a list of the vocabulary words for students. Invite volunteers to identify the compound words on the list. *(campsite, snowcapped, trailhead)* Ask other volunteers to use each of the remaining words in an oral sentence.

TARGET SKILL AND STRATEGY

DRAW CONCLUSIONS Recall with students that when they add together details they have read and with their own related experience to come up with a logical idea, they are drawing a conclusion.

IMPORTANT IDEAS In discussion, have students identify several of the sentences in the book as important ideas or not-so-important ideas. Work with them to make sure they understand the distinction.

ADDITIONAL SKILL INSTRUCTION

MAIN IDEA Point out to students that as they search for the important ideas in a selection, they should be able to find one that is the main idea of the story. Sometimes the main idea of a selection is clear in the title. A fiction story like *Grape Season* often does not have a single main idea.

Name _____

Draw Conclusions

- **Drawing conclusions** means adding what you already know to something you read to make a reasonable decision about something.

Directions Read each passage and answer the questions.

1. Miguel worked hard in Tía Julia's vegetable garden. His parents and sister worked picking grapes. Miguel wasn't old enough to join them in the grape fields. What can you conclude was the attitude of the family toward working? Why did Tía Julia have a garden if the family was so poor?

_____

_____

2. Miguel was eager to go to the fields to pick grapes, but his father said, "Enjoy your freedom now." What conclusion can you draw about Miguel's father's feelings about his job?

_____

_____

3. Miguel wondered why he had never heard of Sequoia National Park, even though he lived only two hours away. Use what you have read about Miguel's life to figure out why.

_____

_____

4. To keep their food safe from bears, Tío Hector brought a big tin box when he and the children went camping. What made Miguel and Luisa realize what a smart thing that was to do?

_____

_____

Vocabulary

Directions Complete each sentence with one of the vocabulary words.

> ### Check the Words You Know
>
> ___campsite   ___crop   ___elevation
> ___migrant workers   ___sequoias   ___snowcapped
> ___trailhead   ___trunk

1. _____ are huge trees that grow in a California park.

2. The park is at a very high _____ in the mountains.

3. Grapes in California are picked by _____.

4. It can be dangerous if bears come to a _____.

5. Many very high mountains are always _____.

6. A very tall tree usually has a huge _____.

7. A large _____ of grapes takes a lot of work for grape pickers.

8. There was a sign at the _____ that showed the route of the trail.

Directions Write two sentences about Miguel and his camping trip. Use as many vocabulary words as you can.

9. _____

_____

10. _____

_____

Grandmother Spider Steals the Sun

SUMMARY This Cherokee myth explains how the Cherokee (and the rest of us) got sun's heat and light. The myth is presented here as a play, illustrated with a class acting it out.

LESSON VOCABULARY

accomplish
commanding
misfortune
quest

chorus
disappeared
perimeter

INTRODUCE THE BOOK

DISCUSS THE TITLE AND AUTHOR Discuss the title and author of *Grandmother Spider Steals the Sun.* Invite students to speculate about the illustration. Ask: Where do you think this tale is taking place? What makes you think so?

BUILD BACKGROUND Remind students that people who lived long ago in cultures around the world made up stories, or myths, to explain to themselves aspects of nature before anyone knew enough science to understand the real reasons.

PREVIEW/USE TEXT FEATURES Have students preview the book by paging through it and looking at the illustrations. Ask: How are pages 3 and 24 different from the rest of the book? How is most of the book presented? Is most of the book fiction or nonfiction? What makes you think as you do?

ELL Make sure all students understand that a play is a story presented in a different form. Help them realize that movies and television shows are plays, or stories acted out.

READ THE BOOK

SET PURPOSE Recall with students that they should use what they learned as they previewed the book to help them set a purpose for reading. Remind them that their purpose might change as they read and discover more about the book.

STRATEGY SUPPORT: INFERRING Recall with students that good readers "read between the lines" to figure out what a myth is trying to explain and why it has the kinds of characters it does. Tell students that they can combine what they read with what they already know to draw a conclusion, but then they can go further to infer a lesson or to interpret what they have read.

COMPREHENSION QUESTIONS

PAGE 3 Are the Cherokee Native Americans? What makes you think so? *(Yes. They lived in what is now the southeast part of the United States.)*

PAGES 4–5 What clues on these pages show that this is a play? *(It lists characters, settings, and staging directions as well as specific directions and dialogue for Scene 1.)* What does the illustration show? *(It shows a class of third-graders putting on the story as a play.)*

PAGES 4–18 What do 'Possum, Buzzard, and Grandmother Spider try to do? *(They all try to bring some of the sun to the people so they don't have to always be in the dark.)*

PAGE 20 Why was Grandmother Spider successful even though the others had failed? *(She was more clever. She was small enough not to be noticed, and she figured out that she should take a pot to protect herself from the heat and light of the piece of sun she wanted to get.)*

REVISIT THE BOOK

READER RESPONSE

1. Students should name the three main characters: 'Possum, who tried to carry the sun in his tail but burned the fur from it; Buzzard, who tried to carry the piece of sun on his head but burned the feathers from it; Grandmother Spider, who successfully took some sun in a pot she made to protect herself from it.

2. Grandmother Spider was successful because she was small enough not to be seen and smart enough to make a pot to carry the sun so she wouldn't be burned.

3. In *disappeared,* the prefix is *dis-* and the base word is *appear* (the *–ed* is an inflectional ending). The base word *appear* is contradicted by the prefix *dis-,* which means "opposite." In *misfortune,* the prefix is *mis-* and the base *fortune.* The meaning of *fortune* is reversed by the meaning of the prefix, which also is "opposite."

4. Cherokee, like most peoples long ago, told myths to try to explain nature. At the time, they did not know the scientific explanations for things.

EXTEND UNDERSTANDING Point out to students that many Native American tribal peoples went through a "Trail of Tears" as they were forced to move far from their homes and to give up their territories.

RESPONSE OPTIONS

DRAMA Encourage students to put on the play. Have small teams work together to do the writing, plan the props and costumes, and so on. All students in the class can participate in the acting, as those who are not named characters can be in the chorus or act as people or wasps. You may want to encourage students to put on the play for another class, perhaps of younger students.

SCIENCE CONNECTION

Provide students with books and other resources to find out about the sun, including how Earth's orbit brings day and night. Encourage them to report their findings and compare the facts to the getting of sunlight as portrayed in the myth.

Skill Work

TEACH/REVIEW VOCABULARY

Work with students to use each vocabulary word in an oral sentence. Encourage them to try to include context clues to the meaning of each word.

TARGET SKILL AND STRATEGY

CHARACTERS, SETTING, PLOT Remind students that *characters* are the people or animals in a story, *setting* is its time and place, and *plot* is what happens. Point out that these are easy to discover in a play, because the author usually specifically names the characters, tells the setting, and describes the action.

INFERRING In discussion, have students infer what kinds of animals lived in the area where the Cherokee did. Ask them to explain why they think as they do.

ADDITIONAL SKILL INSTRUCTION

MAIN IDEA Remind students that the main idea of a story is what the whole story is about. Have them discuss whether the title of this myth tells its main idea.

Name _____

Characters, Setting, Plot

- **Characters** are the people or animals a story is about.
- **Setting** is where and when a story takes place.
- **Plot** is what happens in a story: the beginning, the middle, and the end.

Directions Answer the questions that follow about *Grandmother Spider Steals the Sun*.

1. Some characters in a story are main characters because most the of the action tells about them. Who do you think are the main characters in the story?

_____

2. Some characters are minor characters because they don't have much to do with the action in the story or play. Who are the minor characters in the play?

_____

3. What is the setting of the play? Tell where it takes place. When do you think it took place? Why?

_____

_____

4. Tell what happens in each part of the play.

   Beginning:

   _____

   _____

   Middle:

   _____

   _____

   End:

   _____

   _____

Vocabulary

Directions Write the meaning of each vocabulary word. Use a dictionary if you need to. Then write a sentence that includes each word.

Check the Words You Know

___accomplish   ___chorus   ___commanding
___disappeared   ___misfortune   ___perimeter
___quest
---

1. accomplish _____

_____

2. chorus _____

_____

3. commanding _____

_____

4. disappeared _____

_____

5. misfortune _____

_____

6. perimeter _____

_____

7. quest _____

_____

Animal Tracking: Learn More About Animals

SUMMARY This nonfiction book explores what people can learn about animals by tracking how, when, and where they move. Also included are details about different methods scientists use to better understand animals.

LESSON VOCABULARY

analyze	biologists
classify	data
hibernating	mammal
measurement	migrate
scat	tranquilizers

INTRODUCE THE BOOK

INTRODUCE THE TITLE AND AUTHOR Discuss with students the title and the author of *Animal Tracking: Learn More About Animals*. Based on the title, ask students what kind of information they think this book will provide. Ask: Why do you think the book is called *Animal Tracking: Learn More About Animals?* Direct students to look at the cover illustration and ask them what clues this gives about the selection.

BUILD BACKGROUND Ask students if they have ever seen birds flying south for the winter or returning in the spring and if they know why birds migrate. Discuss with students what they know about other migrating animals and how they know it, such as from documentaries or other sources.

PREVIEW/USE TEXT FEATURES Invite students to skim the book and look through the photographs, illustrations, map, and captions. Ask how these elements give students an idea of the book's organization and content.

READ THE BOOK

SET PURPOSE Have students set a purpose for reading *Animal Tracking: Learn More About Animals*. Students' curiosity about migrating animals or about wildlife in general should guide this purpose. Suggest that as they read, students take notes about the different migrating animals.

STRATEGY SUPPORT: TEXT STRUCTURE Explain to students that the text structure describes and defines different ways to track animals. Suggest that as students read, they us a graphic organizer to list each visited city and the descriptions about each way to track animals.

COMPREHENSION QUESTIONS

PAGE 4 How can you tell if a grizzly bear has been nearby? *(A grizzly rubs against trees to leave a scent. In the process, it strips the bark from the tree and leaves behind fur.)*

PAGES 8–9 What two conclusions can you draw about why biologists might not use radio collars anymore? *(There are many modern methods that scientists use today; it's difficult and dangerous to put collars on bears unless they are hibernating.)*

PAGE 21 What questions do you have about tracking insects? *(Possible response: How does the Doppler radar track them? Do all insects migrate? Where do they migrate?)*

PAGE 21 Why is it important to track migrating animals? *(Possible response: We can learn a lot about the animals and nature.)*

REVISIT THE BOOK
READER RESPONSE
1. Possible response: The diagram helps me visualize how GPS devices work.
2. Possible response: Heading: Tracking Cranes in Planes; Example: Biologists help whooping cranes raised in captivity to migrate south.
3. Possible response: The page talks about microchip transmitters being placed under a snake's skin, so they must be very small. Also the book is about tracking, so it must be some kind of device that helps people track animals.
4. Possible responses: owl scat; scat helps to classify the owls.

EXTEND UNDERSTANDING Remind students that *sequence* is the order in which events occur in a story. Ask students to write down the sequence of tracking one of the animals featured in the selection. Remind them that writing down the sequence can help them remember and summarize what they have read.

RESPONSE OPTIONS
WRITING Ask students to imagine they are an animal being tracked by biologists. Ask them to write a one- to two-page letter to the animal's relatives describing their experiences of being tracked.

SCIENCE CONNECTION
Have students choose a migrating animal and write a short report on where, how, and when the animal migrates. Encourage students to visit the library and use the Internet. Have students present their reports to the class.

Skill Work

TEACH/REVIEW VOCABULARY
After reviewing vocabulary with students, use the words to play several rounds of hangman. Once students guess a word, ask them to supply the definition and use the word in a sentence.

ELL Ask students to skim the text and write down any words they don't understand. Help them find the meanings of these words in the dictionary and prompt them to use the words in sentences.

TARGET SKILL AND STRATEGY
GRAPHIC SOURCES Ask students to read *Animal Tracking: Learn More About Animals.* Suggest that students create two or three graphic organizers to enhance their understanding of the story. For example, they could use a story map for the plot; a time line for the sequence of events; character webs to describe the animal's behaviors; or a problem-and-solution or cause-and-effect chart to understand the action in the story.

TEXT STRUCTURE Review with students that *text structure* is the way text is organized. Point out that the structure of this selection includes descriptions and definition. Remind students that understanding internal text structure can help them pick out the main idea. Suggest they take notes as they read, listing descriptions of each way to track animals.

ADDITIONAL SKILL INSTRUCTION
COMPARE AND CONTRAST Remind students that *comparing* means finding the similarities of things and *contrasting* means finding the differences. Suggest that students compare and contrast cats and dogs, focusing on how animals are alike and how they differ. Graph the findings on the board.

Name _____

Graphic Sources

- **Graphic sources** present information visually and can help you better understand the text.
- Graphic sources include, maps, photographs and captions, time lines, diagrams, graphs, and charts.

Directions Fill in the web below with different details about tracking whooping cranes in planes.

Ways of Tracking

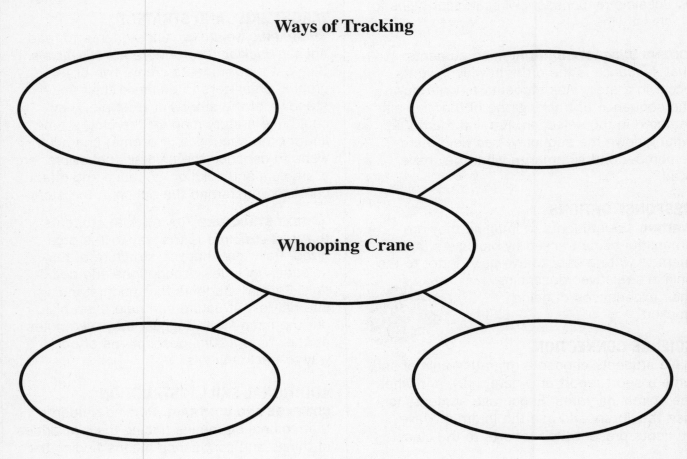

Whooping Crane

1. How did the headings help you understand the story? How did the headings of the story help you fill out the web?

_____

_____

_____

Vocabulary

Directions Circle the letter of the sentence in which the vocabulary word has been used correctly. Then write the definition of the vocabulary word.

> ### Check the Words You Know
>
> ___analyze   ___biologists   ___classify   ___data
> ___hibernating   ___mammal   ___measurement   ___migrate
> ___scat   ___tranquilizers

1. a. The biologists spent three months looking for the information.

    b. Her arteries were clogged with biologists.

_____

2. a. Be careful not to disturb the hibernating bear.

    b. The hibernating bears frolicked in the waterfall and caught fish.

_____

_____

3. a. We collected data about trees for our special report.

    b. Please put the data in the refrigerator where they belong.

_____

4. a. A dinosaur is not a mammal, but a human being is.

    b. I read twenty pages of the mammal.

_____

_____

5. a. Please don't analyze the food into such small pieces.

    b. We need to analyze the information and determine what it means.

_____

_____

Whales and Other Amazing Animals

SUMMARY This book introduces students to the way in which scientists study animals, especially whales. It also introduces readers to scientists' findings about wolves and other canids, gorillas, chimps, and endangered apes.

LESSON VOCABULARY

canids	cetacean
echolocation	flukes
marine biologists	primate
sonar	species

INTRODUCE THE BOOK

INTRODUCE THE TITLE AND AUTHOR Discuss with students the title and the author of *Whales and Other Amazing Animals*. Ask students why a book on animals might have the word *amazing* in its title. Allow them to discuss why or why not animals can be called *amazing*.

BUILD BACKGROUND Discuss students' interest in how scientists approach animals. For instance, marine biologists study why whales beach and how their system of echolocation works. Some scientists go to habitats and observe animals.

PREVIEW/USE TEXT FEATURES Encourage students to look at the captions, sidebars, and charts to get a sense of what animals will be covered in this book. As students look at the photos of the different animals, ask which of the animals they have seen.

ELL Ask students who have had the opportunity to be around animals to volunteer to make up a radio script about these animals. The script should introduce young people to a scientist's way of observing animals.

READ THE BOOK

SET PURPOSE Draw on students' natural interest in animals when asking them to set a purpose for reading the book. They may look at the cover and decide they want to know more about one animal than another. Remind them that nonfiction books often contain much information, so setting a purpose will help keep them focused as they read.

STRATEGY SUPPORT: TEXT STRUCTURE Share with students that good readers should determine how the author organizes the information in the selection. Authors use headings, illustrations, and captions to make information easy to find and read. Ask students how the author organized *Whales and Other Amazing Animals*.

COMPREHENSION QUESTIONS

PAGE 5 Why do many scientists believe that human noise has much to do with why whales beach? *(Human noise and the use of submarine sonar have increased over the years. It is possible that the noises create problems when whales echolocate.)*

PAGES 7, 19 What can be said about animals communicating? *(Whales communicate by echolocation and clicking sounds; some gorillas and chimps communicate with sounds and gestures.)*

PAGE 11 Why are there more coyotes today? *(As the number of wolves decreases, there are fewer to attack coyotes as prey, allowing coyotes to increase.)*

PAGES 12–13 Why are scientists' attempts to put wolves back into the United States working well? *(Scientists are keeping track of where the wolves are; the wolves are reproducing in the wild.)*

REVISIT THE BOOK

READER RESPONSE

1. Possible responses about generalizations: Whales are beached almost every migration season. Many species of whales are endangered. Scientists were concerned about ecosystems becoming unbalanced without as many wolves. Dogs are popular pets.

2. After discussing whales, the author organized the book by discussing types of canids. Responses will vary.

3. The two words are *echo* and *location*. Together, *echolocation* means using a sound to locate something.

4. three kinds of baleen whales: blue, right, humpback

EXTEND UNDERSTANDING As students research endangered species on the Internet and at the library, suggest that they research animals that scientists have prevented from becoming extinct. Read about how scientists and other people, like us, helped this effort.

RESPONSE OPTIONS

WRITING/SPEAKING Suggest that students think about what animal interests them the most from the book. Have them research information from a section of the book and write two paragraphs about that animal. Some students might prefer to give an oral report in pairs on the topic they have researched.

SCIENCE CONNECTION

Invite students to make their own chart of animals and the aspects of them that scientists study. Encourage students to find different ways that scientists study animals, such as observing how whales react to human sounds and teaching animals to communicate. Have students look for ways that are different from those suggested in the book.

Skill Work

TEACH/REVIEW VOCABULARY

As the students read this book, notice which words they find most difficult or intriguing. Students interested in echolocation may want to research the subject and tell the class more about scientists' findings. Some students may be interested in the work of marine biologists and can report on what it takes to be one. Others may research words having to do with canids or other dog-like animals.

TARGET SKILL AND STRATEGY

GENERALIZE Because this reader presents a number of facts and examples about animals, students will need to organize the information in order to *generalize* the topic. To express what the animals have in common, students' generalizations should show likenesses by using clue words such as *many*, *most*, *generally*, *overall*, etc.

TEXT STRUCTURE Tell students that authors use different *text structures*. They can organize the information by subject matter; by chronological, or time, order; or in other ways. Ask: How does the author organize the information in this selection? How does it help you understand the selection?

ADDITIONAL SKILL INSTRUCTION

AUTHOR'S PURPOSE Explain that *author's purpose* is the reason or reasons an author has for writing. Because every author's goal is to communicate, authors often have more than one purpose for writing. Review with students the four typical reasons—to persuade, to inform, to entertain, and to express mood or feeling. Open a discussion by asking what two reasons the author of this book might have had in mind. *(to inform, to entertain)* Ask students to support their answers.

Generalize

- When authors present one statement about many ideas or people, they **generalize**. A generalization is a kind of conclusion.
- Clue words such as *all*, *many*, *none*, and *usually* show a generalization.

Directions For each generalization below, list two facts that support it.
Use *Whales and Other Amazing Animals* to help you.

- There are many ways a whale can end up beached.

1. _____

2. _____

- Many human activities can cause whales to beach.

3. _____

4. _____

- Imbalances in nature generally create problems.

5. _____

6. _____

- Wolves and dogs have many similarities that make them good pets.

7. _____

8. _____

- Many animals other than dogs make interesting pets.

9. _____

10. _____

Vocabulary

Directions Draw a line from each vocabulary word to its definition.

Check the Words You Know

| ___canids | ___cetacean | ___echolocation | ___flukes |
| ___marine biologists | ___primate | ___sonar | ___species |

1. primate

2. species

3. cetacean

4. flukes

5. marine biologists

6. canids

7. sonar

8. echolocation

a. dog-like animals

b. a marine animal that breathes through a blowhole

c. sending out waves to find objects

d. halves of whale's tail

e. a method for detecting sound underwater

f. mammals that are among the most intelligent beings on Earth

g. scientists who study ocean plants and animals

h. a system for classifying animals

Directions Write a paragraph about whales using as many vocabulary words as possible.

_____

_____

_____

_____

_____

_____

_____

Coral Reefs

SUMMARY This nonfiction book about coral reefs identifies what makes up the reefs, tells why coral reefs are important, and suggests ways to protect them.

LESSON VOCABULARY

algae	atoll
colony	coral
coral polyp	coral reef
global warming	lagoon
pollution	tentacle

INTRODUCE THE BOOK

INTRODUCE THE TITLE AND AUTHOR Discuss the title and author of *Coral Reefs*. Invite students to consider the cover photograph. Ask: Do you think this is a coral reef? Might those be different kinds of coral?

BUILD BACKGROUND Briefly discuss with students what they know about the dangers to people, animals, and plants from pollution. Explain that the ocean is not immune. Some ocean animals and plants are also endangered by pollution.

PREVIEW/USE TEXT FEATURES Have students preview the book by paging through it and looking at the photos. Ask: How can captions and labels help you understand what's in a photograph or diagram? How can the glossary help you?

ELL Make sure students understand that words highlighted in the text are in the glossary. If they cannot figure out the meaning of a highlighted word, they can look it up in the glossary at the back of the book.

READ THE BOOK

SET PURPOSE Ask students to discuss what they think their purpose for reading *Coral Reefs* could be. Remind them to base their ideas on what they saw as they previewed the book.

STRATEGY SUPPORT: PREDICT AND SET PURPOSE In discussion, recall with students why it is important to predict what they think a book might be about and to set a purpose for reading. Remind them that previewing can help on both counts.

COMPREHENSION QUESTIONS

PAGE 3 What is a coral reef? (*An undersea ridge of hard rock formed by tiny animals called corals.*)

PAGES 4–5 What is the main difference between hard and soft corals? (*Soft corals do not have a hard outer skeleton the way hard corals do, so soft corals are not part of coral reefs.*)

PAGE 8 What are the three main kinds of coral reefs? (*fringing reefs, barrier reefs, and atolls*)

PAGE 11 Why should we make an effort to protect coral reefs? (*The reefs protect nearby land and provide food and refuge for many plants and animals.*)

PAGES 19–21 How can people protect the reefs? (*create marine parks, plant mangrove trees and other plants, reduce global warming, and do reef checks*)

REVISIT THE BOOK

READER RESPONSE

1. Dangers coral reefs face (Causes) include dynamite fishing, pollution, global warming, tourists, and building close to shore. Effects of all these include damage to the reefs. Dynamite fishing and pollution kill plants and animals in the reef; global warming raises the water temperature, which kills the algae and starves the coral until it dies; people break the coral and demand to buy it; even wearing sunscreen when swimming in the ocean poisons plants and animals in a reef.

2. Responses will vary, but most students will realize that the coral reefs could all die, which would have an impact on the shores by the oceans.

3. Pollution means adding dirty and dangerous substances to something such as air or water. Pollution can kill not only the coral reefs but also the animals and plants that live in them.

4. Possible response: We must protect the coral reefs because we depend on them. They protect the nearby land from storms. They are home for many plants and animals. They provide food and medicine.

EXTEND UNDERSTANDING Explain that there are other kinds of reefs, some in lakes or other bodies of water. They are narrow ridges of rock or sand at or near the surface of water.

RESPONSE OPTIONS

ART Have students draw or paint a mural of a coral reef. You may want to have them look at other sources of information to get accurate pictures of animals and plants in coral reefs. Ask them to label the reef and plants and animals in it, as well as nearby land. They may want to share and explain the mural to another class.

SCIENCE CONNECTION

Provide research materials such as books, encyclopedias, and the Internet, so students can find out more about coral and coral polyps. Have them follow the directions on pages 22–23 to make models of coral polyps. You may want to challenge them to figure out other materials to use to make the model. Have them stick several model polyps together to form a model of a coral reef.

Skill Work

TEACH/REVIEW VOCABULARY

Read the vocabulary words. Have students locate each vocabulary word in the text where it is highlighted. Ask them to identify the context clues they find to the word's meaning and compare them to the definitions given in the Glossary on page 24.

TARGET SKILL AND STRATEGY

CAUSE AND EFFECT Remind students that an *effect* is something that happens and a *cause* it what makes it happen. Ask volunteers to provide some oral examples, including from the book.

PREDICT AND SET PURPOSE Invite students to tell you how predicting what they are about to read and setting a purpose for reading can help them be better readers.

ADDITIONAL SKILL INSTRUCTION

GENERALIZE Discuss with students that generalizing means coming up with an idea that covers many things without being specific about any one of them. Invite volunteers to offer one or two generalizations about all coral reefs.

Cause and Effect

- A **cause** tells what makes something happen.
- An **effect** is what happens after a cause.

Directions Answer the questions that follow about *Coral Reefs*.

1. Why don't soft corals help build coral reefs?

_____

2. Why do soft corals live in deeper water than hard corals?

_____

3. What makes a coral polyp go inside itself?

_____

4. Why are most coral reefs in the tropics and not farther away from the Equator?

_____

_____

5. What are two causes of danger to the coral reefs?

_____

_____

_____

6. What are two ways to help protect the coral reefs?

_____

_____

_____

Name _____

Vocabulary

Directions Write a sentence that includes each word. Try to use a context clue to its meaning. Use the glossary to check the word's meaning if you need to.

┌───┐
│ **Check the Words You Know** │
│ ___algae   ___atoll   ___colony │
│ ___coral   ___coral polyp   ___coral reef │
│ ___global warming ___lagoon   ___pollution │
│ ___tentacle │
└───┘

1. algae

_____

2. atoll

_____

3. colony

_____

4. coral

_____

5. coral polyp

_____

6. coral reef

_____

7. global warming

_____

8. Write a sentence using two or more vocabulary words.

_____

_____

Extraordinary Athletes

SUMMARY In this essay, attention is given to three impressive people whose talent and determination have made them extraordinary athletes despite serious physical disabilities. Jean Driscoll is a wheelchair marathon runner. Oscar Pistorius is a champion runner despite having no legs and running on "blades." Erik Weihenmayer is blind but has climbed all Seven Summits—the highest mountain on each of Earth's continents.

LESSON VOCABULARY

advantage	amputated
determination	disabilities
marathon	qualified
summit	ultimate

INTRODUCE THE BOOK

INTRODUCE THE TITLE AND AUTHOR Discuss the title and author of *Extraordinary Athletes*. Draw attention to the photograph and ask what might make the mountain climber extraordinary.

ELL Help students decode the word *extraordinary* by pointing out the prefix *extra-*, which means "outside, beyond what is normal or expected." Brainstorm with students to name other words with the prefix, such as *extracurricular, extrasensory, extraterritorial,* and *extravehicular.* Have students check a dictionary for the meanings.

BUILD BACKGROUND Explain that many disabled people are able to do amazing things, including competing in sports. Point out that the Paralympics, in which disabled people compete, takes place with the regular Olympics.

PREVIEW/USE TEXT FEATURES Have students preview the book. Invite them to discuss text features such as captions, headings, and highlighted words. Point out the Glossary on page 24 and the suggestion for a debate on pages 22–23.

READ THE BOOK

SET PURPOSE Recall with students that this book is nonfiction. Ask volunteers to name their purpose for reading. Remind students that they may change their purpose as they read to suit what they find.

STRATEGY SUPPORT: SUMMARIZE Recall with students that good readers often summarize the main ideas of what they are reading as they go along in order to check their understanding. Tell students that after they finish reading a section, they should take a few minutes to summarize what they have read.

COMPREHENSION QUESTIONS

PAGE 3 Why does the author think all top athletes are amazing? *(Those who reach the top have trained hard for many years.)* What makes the three described in this book even more amazing? *(All are disabled and had to overcome their own special difficulties.)*

PAGES 5–6 Jean Driscoll never dreamed she could participate in sports. What inspired her to get started playing wheelchair sports? *(A friend encouraged her to try wheelchair soccer. She enjoyed it so much she began to play other sports.)*

PAGES 10–11 What are Oscar Pistorius's "blades"? *(They are the special j-shaped running prosthetics Oscar wears when he is racing.)*

PAGES 11–12 What problem did Oscar cause other Olympic runners? *(Oscar could run so fast on his "blades" that normal runners argued he had a special advantage.)*

PAGE 18 Although Erik Weihenmayer is blind, he depends on other talents when he is climbing mountains. What helps him? *(his strength, balance, and senses of touch and hearing)*

REVISIT THE BOOK

READER RESPONSE

1. Responses will vary, but many students will generalize that physically challenged athletes must work harder than ordinary athletes and are often more motivated to succeed.

2. Main accomplishments—Jean Driscoll: led her college basketball team to two national championships, earned four medals at the 1988 Paralympics, won the women's wheelchair division of the Boston Marathon, won more Boston Marathon records than anyone else. Oscar Pistorius: began breaking world records as soon as he began to run on his "blades," won many medals at the 2004 Summer Paralympics, competed against non-disabled runners but was not allowed to do that in the Olympics; Erik Weihenmayer: climbed many mountains, beginning with Mount Everest and continuing to conquer all Seven Summits.

3. Sentences will vary. Not all vocabulary words need be used in each story.

4. Responses will vary, but have students explain their choices.

EXTEND UNDERSTANDING Special prosthetics like Oscar's "blades" are often used to allow those with disabilities to participate in sports. There are also many wheelchair adaptations for various kinds of sports. Have students note the special racing wheelchair Jean uses in the photograph on page 9.

RESPONSE OPTIONS

LANGUAGE ARTS/DEBATE Have students follow the directions on pages 22–23 to hold a debate about Oscar Pistorius's use of his special "blades" in races. You may want to have students work in teams rather than in pairs to do the research and carry out the debate.

SOCIAL STUDIES CONNECTION

Invite interested students to do some research into the Olympic Games and the Paralympic Games. How are the athletes who participate in both games chosen? What are some of the sports included in both games? Ask students to report the results of their research to the class, either orally or in a written paragraph or two.

Skill Work

TEACH/REVIEW VOCABULARY
Using the list of vocabulary words in the Glossary on page 24, have students brainstorm to include each word in a sentence about a topic not covered in the book.

TARGET SKILL AND STRATEGY
GENERALIZE Remind students that they may come across generalizations in their reading that are statements that cover many ideas. Sometimes generalizations are identified with clue words such as *all, most, never, usually, generally,* and so on. Generalizations should be supported by observable facts or statements.

SUMMARIZE Remind students that they can help themselves remember what they read by summarizing the main ideas of each section before proceeding to the next one.

ADDITIONAL SKILL INSTRUCTION
GRAPHIC SOURCES Have students discuss the help that they get from graphics such as captions, headings, illustrations, and photographs.

Generalize

- A **generalization** is a broad statement that applies to many examples.
- Sometimes a generalization is signaled by a clue word such as *all, most, many, never, usually,* or *generally.*
- A generalization should be supported by facts and be reasonable.
- A generalization can include your own background knowledge.

Directions Consider what you read in *Extraordinary Athletes.* Follow the directions below.

1. Write a generalization about disabled athletes.

_____

_____

2. List facts and statements from the book that support your generalization. Add something from your own background knowledge if you choose to.

_____

_____

_____

3. Write a generalization about special opportunities for disabled athletes to compete.

_____

_____

4. List facts and statements from the book that support your generalization. Add something from your own background knowledge if you choose to.

_____

_____

_____

Vocabulary

Directions Write the word from the box that best matches each clue.

Check the Words You Know
___advantage ___amputated ___determination
___disabilities ___marathon ___qualified
___summit ___ultimate

1. the very top _____

2. cut off _____

3. a long race _____

4. limiting conditions _____

5. makes it easier to do things _____

6. will to succeed _____

Directions Think about the words. Write one or more words that fit each description.

7. adjective, or word that describes things _____

8. a word with a prefix _____

9. past tense verb _____

10. word with three syllables _____

Directions Write two sentences about one or more of the athletes in the book. Use as many vocabulary words as you can.

_____

_____

_____

_____

Largest, Fastest, Lightest, Longest

SUMMARY *Largest, Fastest, Lightest, Longest* tells the story of *Guinness World Records,* the famous compendium of trivia. This nonfiction reader describes how the book originated, how records are verified and entered into the book, and what sorts of records the book contains.

LESSON VOCABULARY

accomplishment	compendium
existing	procedure
superlative	translated
trivia	verified

INTRODUCE THE BOOK

INTRODUCE THE TITLE AND AUTHOR Discuss with students the title and the author of *Largest, Fastest, Lightest, Longest.* First, talk about what the words in the main title all have in common. Then, have students read the subtitle, The *Guinness World Records* Story, and invite students to tell what they know about *Guinness World Records.*

BUILD BACKGROUND Discuss with students the meaning of the word *record.* Ask students to name any famous records they know. *(Possible responses: Tallest mountain is Everest; Barry Bonds holds the record for most homeruns in a baseball season.)* Talk with students about how these records are measured. Have students suggest records that might be hard to check, such as the oldest person, and explain why they think checking the record would be difficult. Then discuss where a person might look for records such as these.

PREVIEW/USE TEXT FEATURES If students are unfamiliar with *Guinness World Records,* explain that this reader is about a book that contains thousands of records in many categories. Have students skim through the reader and look at the pictures and captions. Ask: What sorts of records does this reader talk about?

READ THE BOOK

SET PURPOSE To help students set purposes for reading, invite them to think of one question that they would like to ask about *Guinness World Records.* Have students read to find answers to their questions.

STRATEGY SUPPORT: IMPORTANT IDEAS Explain to students that *important ideas* are the essential ideas presented in a selection, the supporting details for those ideas, and specific information of facts that provide insight into an author's purpose for writing. Tell students that in a nonfiction selection, special fonts, illustrations, or signal words and phrases are used.

COMPREHENSION QUESTIONS

PAGE 4 Besides informing the reader, what do you think is the author's purpose for showing the largest spider on a ruler? *(Possible response: entertaining the reader)*

PAGE 6 The sizes of birds' eggs are compared on this page. What else does the author compare or contrast? *(She contrasts Earth's coldest temperature with its average temperature.)*

PAGES 8–9 What questions do you still have after reading these pages? Where could you look for answers? *(Possible responses: What are some of the languages that* Guinness World Records *is translated into? I could look in the library or in some part of the book itself. It might mention other languages.)*

PAGES 16–18 What steps would you need to take to get into *Guinness World Records? (think of a record to set or break, write to* Guinness World Records *and describe your idea, wait for them to write and accept your idea)*

REVISIT THE BOOK

READER RESPONSE

1. Possible response: I don't think photographs could have done as good a job because a photograph shows only one thing at a time. The illustrations seemed to tell little stories on their own.
2. Responses will vary.
3. Super; Possible response: *Super* means the best. *Superlative* means something with the best qualities.
4. Possible responses:
   Page and item—4, largest spider; 4, fastest fish; 5, lightest bird egg; 5, coldest temperature; 11, rainiest place on Earth; 12, heaviest hailstone; 13, largest number of tap dancers dancing at one time; 15, largest dog ears

EXTEND UNDERSTANDING Have students look through the pictures in the reader once again. Point out that even though this is a nonfiction book, the illustrations look like cartoons. Discuss with students why drawings like these may have been used and how the illustrations add to their understanding or enjoyment of the book.

RESPONSE OPTIONS

WRITING Have students think of records that they would like to set for *Guinness World Records.* Provide students with one or two copies of the book and tell them to check whether their ideas are already in the record book. Then have students write out their ideas on copies of the *Guinness World Record* idea forms. Have students share their ideas.

SCIENCE CONNECTION

Have students make a class list of some natural records they expect to find in *Guinness World Records,* such as driest place, greatest snowfall, most hurricanes. Have students make predictions about what parts of the world will hold these records and put them on a chart. Then have students check the records in the book. Tell them to plot the locations of these "bests" on a map of the world and list them in their natural records chart. Discuss as a class which predictions were correct and which incorrect and which records were most surprising.

Skill Work

TEACH/REVIEW VOCABULARY
Read through the Glossary with students. Pair students and have each partner write three clues for each word. Clues can be definitions, parts of speech, pronunciations, synonyms, antonyms, or spelling. Then have partners exchange clues and try to guess the words without using the Glossary.

TARGET SKILL AND STRATEGY

GRAPHIC SOURCES Remind students that *graphic sources* are maps, charts, graphs, photos with captions—ways of showing information visually. Tell students that they should use these graphics as they read to help them make sense of the text. Have them choose a graphic source from the book and tell about it. They should tell how it made the text easier to understand.

ELL Have students complete a *Comparison and Contrast Chart* with the following column headings: *Record: How Record Was Measured; Nature, Animal, or Human Record.* Help students complete the chart for two records in the reader.

IMPORTANT IDEAS Remind students that important ideas are details that give a reader insight into an author's purpose for writing. After reading, ask: What was the author's purpose for writing this selection? What ideas support the author's purpose for writing? How did the structure of the selection help you understand theses ideas?

ADDITIONAL SKILL INSTRUCTION

AUTHOR'S PURPOSE Review with students that an *author's purpose* is the author's reason for writing a text. Remind students that while many nonfiction authors write with the purpose of informing the reader about something, they may also write with another purpose: to entertain, persuade, or express. As they read, have students figure out what other purpose Kirsten Anderson may have had, besides informing the reader, for writing *Largest, Fastest, Lightest, Longest.*

Name _____

Graphic Sources

- **Graphic sources** present information visually and can help you better understand the text.
- Graphic sources include maps, photographs and captions, time lines, diagrams, graphs, and charts.

Directions Use *Largest, Fastest, Lightest, Longest* to answer the following questions.

1. Reread pages 7–8. What does the illustration suggest might be the answer to the question Sir Hugh Beaver tried to answer in 1951?

_____

_____

2. What do you think the illustration on pages 8–9 is meant to indicate?

_____

_____

3. How does the illustration on page 11 make it easier to understand the text on that page?

_____

_____

4. What record do you think the illustration at the top of page 13 tells about?

_____

_____

5. What is the illustration on page 18 about?

_____

_____

Vocabulary

Directions Choose a word from the word box that has the same meaning as the underlined words. Write the word on the line.

Check the Words You Know

___accomplishment   ___compendium   ___existing
___procedure   ___superlative   ___translated
___trivia   ___verified

1. I like to read books that contain <u>fun and amusing facts</u>. _____

2. The <u>book that gave a lot of information in a small space</u> took a long time to read.

_____

3. The runner's world record could not be <u>proved true</u>. _____

4. You should be very proud of your <u>special thing that you did</u>.

_____

5. A <u>way of doing something</u> should be followed carefully in a science experiment.

_____

Directions For each word or phrase below, choose a word from the word box that has the opposite meaning. Write the word on the line.

6. proved false _____

7. average _____

8. failure _____

9. in the same language _____

10. extinct _____

Gemstones Around the World

SUMMARY *Gemstones Around the World* describes the twelve gemstones that serve as traditional birthstones. This nonfiction reader includes pictures of each gem, descriptions of its qualities, and details about where the gem is found in the world.

LESSON VOCABULARY

birthstone	brilliant	crystal
flaws	mined	minerals
quartz	rockhounds	transparent

INTRODUCE THE BOOK

INTRODUCE THE TITLE AND AUTHOR Discuss with students the title and the author of *Gemstones Around the World.* Ask students if they recognize the stone in the cover photograph. (diamond) Point out the content triangle, and talk about why a book featuring diamonds would relate to science.

BUILD BACKGROUND Put the word *gem* at the center of a content web. Invite students to suggest all the words that come to mind when they think of the word *gem.* Suggest that they think not only about the finished product, but where gems come from. Then tell students that the selection they are about to read will describe some well-known gems.

PREVIEW/USE TEXT FEATURES Have students look through the pictures, charts, and map in the book. Ask what students expect to learn from the book about gems. *(information about the twelve birthstones that belong to each month, where the birthstones are found, how they are formed)*

ELL Invite students to talk about gems that are found in their home countries or that are important to their families' cultures. Have volunteers describe the gems and why they are considered special or valuable to their families and friends.

READ THE BOOK

SET PURPOSE Use the Prior Knowledge activity to guide students to set a purpose for reading. Remind students to think about what they would like to know about gems and birthstones. Then have them choose what they would most like to learn, and invite them to read to find out more about this topic.

STRATEGY SUPPORT: INFERRING Before reading, discuss with students what they know about gemstones. Ask them what they think they will learn from reading this selection. Remind students that it is important to combine what they know with what they read to create new information and better understand the text.

COMPREHENSION QUESTIONS

PAGE 4 What is the effect of cutting and polishing gemstones? (makes them sparkle and shine)

PAGES 6–7 Make a generalization about where gemstones are found. *(Possible response: Many gemstones are found in the southern part of Africa.)*

PAGE 11 What prior knowledge helped you understand the information on this page? *(Possible response: I know what a diamond looks like, so I could imagine how hard it is.)*

PAGE 14 Why do you think there is a picture of the British Crown Jewels on this page? *(Possible response: The page is about rubies, so there are probably rubies in the Crown Jewels.)*

PAGE 19 What generalization does the author make on this page? *(Most of the blue topaz that we see today has been treated with light.)*

REVISIT THE BOOK

READER RESPONSE

1. Response will vary but should include facts and opinions.
2. Responses will vary but should show use of background knowledge and understanding of text.
3. Possible responses: My grandmother wore her stunning birthstone ring to the opera. The rockhound searched for shiny, green emeralds in North Carolina.
4. Africa and Asia

EXTEND UNDERSTANDING

Have students analyze the structure of the sections in pages 8–19 to identify how each section is set up. Elicit that each section consists of a photograph of the gemstone, its name and related month, textual discussion of the gemstone that identifies where it is found, and another photograph that highlights an interesting fact about the gemstone.

RESPONSE OPTIONS

VIEWING Show students images of some of the precious gems at the Smithsonian Museum of Natural History, including the Hope Diamond and the British Crown jewels. Have students write brief paragraphs describing which gems are their favorites and why.

SCIENCE CONNECTION

Explain to students that geologists are people who study the physical nature of the earth and rocks. Tell students to imagine that they are geologists. Have each student choose a gem described in the text, such as their birthstone, and find out how their gem is formed.

Skill Work

TEACH/REVIEW VOCABULARY

Read through the Glossary with students. Have each student find a picture of his or her birthstone in the reader. Ask students to use the pictures and the vocabulary words to write paragraphs describing their stones.

TARGET SKILL AND STRATEGY

FACT AND OPINION Tell students that a statement of *fact* is a statement that can be proven true or false; a statement of *opinion* is someone's viewpoint. Explain that facts can be proven true or false by checking in books; by observing, weighing, or measuring; or by consulting an expert. Invite students to think of a statement of fact or a statement of opinion to share with the class. Ask the class to decide if the statement is a fact or opinion.

INFERRING Tell students that *inferring* is combining background knowledge with what they have read to create new information. Ask: What do you know about gemstones? What did you read about gemstones? What new ideas did this lead to?

ADDITIONAL SKILL INSTRUCTION

CAUSE AND EFFECT Review with students that an effect is what happens and a cause is why that event happens. To figure out the cause of something, a reader may have to ask questions such as "Why did this probably happen?" Have students think about the qualities of the gems described in the book, and tell them to suggest what caused these gemstones to be assigned as birthstones.

Name _____

Fact and Opinion

- When you read nonfiction, you will read some sentences that contain statements of **fact** and others that contain statements of **opinion.** Facts can be proved true or false. Opinions are statements of ideas and feelings. They cannot be proved.

Directions Read the following sentences from *Gemstones Around the World.* Write whether each one is a fact or an opinion, and explain why.

1. A birthstone is a gem that has been assigned to a certain month.

_____

2. Gemstones are like snowflakes because no two are the same.

_____

3. Brilliant cut sapphire is much more appealing than a pear cut garnet.

_____

4. Blue topaz is only found in Asia.

_____

5. The best miners are ants because they bring anthill garnets to the surface of an anthill.

_____

6. Aquamarine means "seawater" in Latin.

_____

7. Colorless diamonds can split light into the colors of the rainbow.

_____

8. Rockhounds from North Carolina have an exciting hobby!

_____

9. Pieces of peridot have been found in meteors that have crashed into Earth!

_____

10. The Roebling Opal is one of the world's largest opals.

Name _____

Vocabulary

Directions Use eight words from the box to complete the puzzle below.

Check the Words You Know

___birthstone	___brilliant	___crystal	___flaws
___mined	___minerals	___quartz	___rockhounds
___transparent			

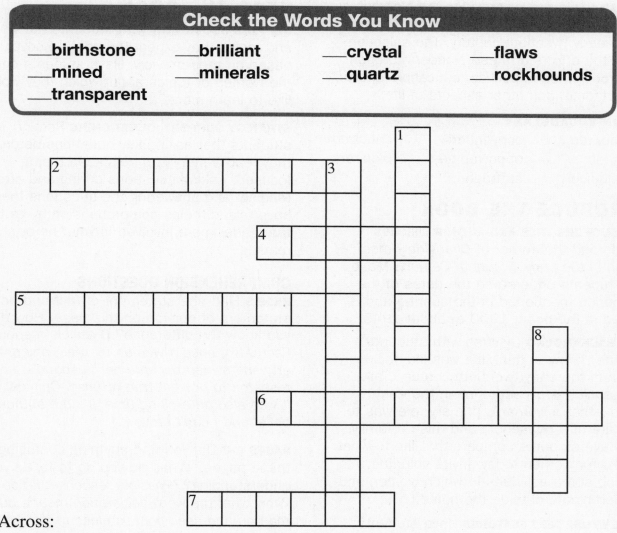

Across:

2. very bright and shiny

4. defects or blemishes

5. the nickname given to people who hunt, dig, and collect rocks and gems

6. a gemstone associated with one of the twelve months of the year

7. a very hard mineral found in many different types of rock

Down:

1. a hard, solid piece of some substance that is naturally formed of flat surfaces and angles

3. allowing light to pass through

8. dug up from under the ground

Changing Times

SUMMARY This reader provides the biographies of many women who broke down barriers during the early twentieth century. The selection details the efforts of these pioneers to open doors for women in politics, education, sports, the workforce, and other aspects of life.

LESSON VOCABULARY

accepted	convention	criticized
limited	opportunities	pioneers
prejudiced	suffrage	

INTRODUCE THE BOOK

INTRODUCE THE TITLE AND AUTHOR Discuss the title and the author of *Changing Times: Women in the Early Twentieth Century*. Make sure students understand the dates of the time period mentioned in the subtitle and covered in the book: 1900 to about 1945.

BUILD BACKGROUND Discuss with students what they know or think life was like for women in the early twentieth century. Talk about society's expectations in the early 1900s—that a woman's primary role was to take care of a household and raise a family. Then have students compare that life to what it is like for women today. Invite volunteers to describe some activities in which women and girls participate outside the home.

PREVIEW/USE TEXT FEATURES Have students skim through the book, focusing on the *headings*, *sidebars*, *pictures*, and *captions*. Ask students if they recognize any of the women in the pictures. Discuss with students what they think the book will be about, based on these pictures and the topics mentioned in the headings, captions, and sidebars.

ELL Invite volunteers to describe some of the women pioneers from their own cultures. Provide some examples from students' home countries if students cannot think of examples themselves.

READ THE BOOK

SET PURPOSE Review with students the women and topics they expect the book to cover, based on their preview. Have students choose the women or topics about which they would like to learn more.

STRATEGY SUPPORT: QUESTIONING Remind students that asking key questions before they read a story can help keep them focused. Asking questions during and after reading, and answering the questions they have raised, helps comprehension by getting the reader more involved in what he or she is reading.

COMPREHENSION QUESTIONS

PAGE 3 Find one statement of fact and one statement of opinion on this page. How do you know the difference? *(Possible responses: Fact: Also, once a woman married, any property she owned became her husband's. I can research to prove it true or false. Opinion: But it was also an exciting time. It's the author's belief and I can't prove it.)*

PAGES 6–7 Did you find anything confusing on these pages? What did you do to fix up your understanding? *(Possible response: I didn't know what the word declaration meant, but I read on and used context clues to guess that it meant a document that states ideas.)*

PAGES 12–13 What is one generalization the author makes? *(Possible response: Most doctors were still men.)*

PAGE 16 What statement of opinion does the author make about some women in the early 1900s? *(Possible response: Women pioneers did amazing things.)*

PAGES 18–19 Name one statement of fact in these pages. Where could you check to prove the statement true or false? *(Possible response: At the 1932 Olympics, Babe won two gold medals and one silver in track and field. I could check the information about Babe in an encyclopedia or on the Internet.)*

REVIST THE BOOK

READER RESPONSE

1. Possible responses: Facts: In 1900, women could not vote. Elizabeth Cady Stanton started the Women's Rights Movement. Opinions: Women should stay home with children. Women were not as smart as men.
2. Responses will vary but should show understanding of the text.
3. Responses will vary but should include multiple vocabulary words used properly.
4. Possible response: Elizabeth Cady Stanton, because she helped plan the first Women's Rights Convention in 1848 and wrote its "Declaration of Sentiments."

EXTEND UNDERSTANDING Point out that authors of nonfiction often use headings to help readers understand information or recognize the main idea of a section. Review with students the headings in the book and discuss how the headings help the reader understand the information in each section and recognize the author's main ideas.

RESPONSE OPTIONS

WRITING AND SPEAKING Have each student choose one of the women featured in the book and imagine that she is receiving a "Woman of the Century" award. Direct each student to write a speech introducing the person and explaining why she is a good choice for the award. Have students give their speeches to the class.

SOCIAL STUDIES CONNECTION

Time For SOCIAL STUDIES

Have students research and write biographies of other twentieth century pioneers. Tell students that subjects may be women, African Americans, young people, leaders in a field, or anyone else who was the first to accomplish something important.

Skill Work

TEACH/REVIEW VOCABULARY

Read through the Glossary with students. Direct students to think about whether each word makes them think of happy, positive ideas or unhappy, negative ideas. As a class, have students group the words based on whether they have positive or negative connotations. Tell students to explain their decisions.

TARGET SKILL AND STRATEGY

FACT AND OPINION Explain to students that a *statement of fact* can be proved true or false and can be checked by looking in reference sources, by asking an expert, or even by observing. A *statement of opinion* is a person's beliefs or ideas about something. Point out to students that opinions often contain clue words such as *I believe, in my opinion, best, worst, most, should,* and other judgment words. Give examples of statements of fact and statements of opinion, and discuss with students how to distinguish between the two. Direct students to look for facts and opinions in the text.

QUESTIONING Share with students that they can ask questions to compare and contrast topics in the story. Suggest that students ask themselves questions as they read to help them better understand the text.

ADDITIONAL SKILL INSTRUCTION

GENERALIZE Review with students that when they *generalize*, they are making a broad statement that applies to a group of things or ideas. Provide students with some generalizations and clue words, such as *every, all, most, few, never.* As they read, have students find generalizations that the author makes.

Name _____

Fact and Opinion

- A statement of **fact** is a statement that can be proved true or false. You can check a statement of fact by looking in reference sources, asking an expert, or observing.
- A statement of **opinion** is a person's beliefs or ideas about something. You cannot prove whether it is true or false.

Directions Use the book *Changing Times* to answer the questions below.

1. Reread page 4 in the book. What is a statement of fact on this page?

_____

_____

2. What is one statement of opinion that the author makes on page 4? How do you know that this is an opinion and not a fact?

_____

_____

_____

3. Reread the section of the book entitled "Women in College." What is one statement of fact that the author makes about colleges for women in the 1800s?

_____

4. What is a statement of opinion that the author makes about women in college during the early 1900s?

_____

_____

5. Reread the Conclusion, beginning on page 20 in the reader. Which statement contains both a fact and an opinion? Which part is which?

_____

_____

_____

Vocabulary

Directions For each word below, separate the word into its base word and its ending. Then write a sentence using the base word. Use a dictionary to help you.

1. prejudiced

Base word _____

Ending _____

Sentence with base word _____

_____

2. criticized

Base word _____

Ending _____

Sentence with base word _____

_____

3. accepted

Base word _____

Ending _____

Sentence with base word _____

_____

4. opportunities

Base word _____

Ending _____

Sentence with base word _____

_____

5. limited

Base word _____

Ending _____

Sentence with base word _____

_____

Directions Imagine you are a woman attending the first Women's Rights Convention in 1848. On a separate sheet of paper, write a diary entry about your experience there using the words *convention, pioneers, prejudiced,* and *suffrage.*

Toby the Smart Dog

CAUSE AND EFFECT
MONITOR AND CLARIFY

SUMMARY This story, about a boy wanting to teach his dog Toby to sit, shows students that dogs can learn to do some things but that other things are done by natural instinct.

LESSON VOCABULARY

brightened	commanded
familiar	promise
scampered	suspicious
trotted	twitched

INTRODUCE THE BOOK

INTRODUCE THE TITLE AND AUTHOR Discuss the title and author of *Toby the Smart Dog* with students. Ask students, based on the cover illustration and the title, what they think this story is about.

BUILD BACKGROUND Ask students if they have ever had a dog or a pet or if they have known someone who had a dog or a pet. Discuss what students know about how and what animals learn.

PREVIEW Invite students to look through the story illustrations. Ask students how the illustrations give them an idea of what the story is about. Direct students' attention to the illustration on pages 22–23. Ask students if they think this drawing indicates that there will be a happy ending to the story.

READ THE BOOK

SET PURPOSE Have students set a purpose for reading *Toby the Smart Dog*. Students' curiosity about dogs and their natural instincts should guide their purpose.

STRATEGY SUPPORT: MONITOR AND CLARIFY Explain to students the importance of *monitoring* their understanding as they read. Tell students that there are different ways to *clarify,* or fix, a comprehension problem. Suggest that students write notes about what is happening in the story. They can track the story and check their notes if they encounter a roadblock as they read. Also share with students that if they are asked a question about the story, they can reread to view information they may have forgotten.

COMPREHENSION QUESTIONS

PAGE 5 What story detail makes you think that Charlie may not be able to teach Toby a trick? *(Toby dug up the flowers.)*

PAGES 6–7 Which plot events are important on these pages, and which plot events are not? *(Possible responses: Important: Training Toby was Charlie's biggest goal. Charlie tried to teach Toby to sit. Toby failed but didn't give up. Unimportant: It had taken Mom and Dad a long time to let Charlie have a dog. Charlie met lots of dogs at the shelter.)*

PAGE 13 What details show you the kind of person Charlie was? *(Possible responses: He was responsible because he cleaned up his dog's digging. He was sensitive because he didn't get angry with Toby.)*

PAGE 23 What do you think the author wants you to know and understand about natural instinct and learning? *(Possible responses: I think the author wants me to know that dogs can learn some things, but they do other things by instinct. Sometimes instinct can help a dog to learn.)*

REVISIT THE BOOK

READER RESPONSE

1. Toby was chasing a squirrel.
2. Responses will vary but should include a clarifying strategy such as: rereading, reading on, or taking notes.
3. Words should be used as adverbs, and sentences should demonstrate understanding of vocabulary.
4. Possible responses: sit, walk alongside owner (heel), stop walking, roll over, not jump on people, not beg for food

EXTEND UNDERSTANDING Remind students that a character is a person or animal who takes part in the events of a story. Suggest that students make a character web about Charlie. Putting Charlie's name in the center circle, have students write events in the story that show what Charlie does, what Charlie says, and what others say about Charlie. Based on the finished character web, ask students to discuss what they know about Charlie and to predict what Charlie might do next.

RESPONSE OPTIONS

WRITING Invite students to pretend they are Toby the dog and have them write a letter to Charlie explaining why it seemed to take so long to learn the things Charlie wanted.

SOCIAL STUDIES CONNECTION

Time For
SOCIAL STUDIES

Suggest that students research and write about how seeing eye dogs are trained and how they bond with their visually impaired owners.

Skill Work

TEACH/REVIEW VOCABULARY

Scramble the spelling of each vocabulary word and write the scrambled words on the chalkboard in one column. In another column write the definitions in a different order. Have students unscramble each word and copy its correct definition from the chalkboard.

ELL For each vocabulary word, give students a sentence where the vocabulary word is used correctly and one where it is used incorrectly. Have the student choose the correct sentence.

TARGET SKILL AND STRATEGY

CAUSE AND EFFECT Explain to students that an *effect* is something that happens and a *cause* is why it happens. Model using page 8. Say: After reading page 8, I ask "What happened?" Charlie rode his bike to the library. "Why did it happen?" Charlie wanted to learn how to train Toby. Have students use a cause-and-effect graphic organizer to keep track as they read. Tell students to ask themselves "What happened?" and "Why did it happened?"

MONITOR AND CLARIFY Explain to students that *monitoring* their reading means keeping track of the parts of the story they don't understand. *Clarifying* is using strategies, such as taking notes, reading on, and rereading, to fix the problem.

ADDITIONAL SKILL INSTRUCTION

CHARACTER AND SETTING Remind students that a character is the person or animal that does the actions in the story, and that setting is the time and place where the story occurs. Remind students that the setting of a story can influence how a character behaves. Suggest that, as they read, students make notes about how the setting influences what Charlie does.

Cause and Effect

- A **cause** is why something happened. An **effect** is what happened. Look for clue words such as *because, so, it, then,* and *since.*

Directions Reread the passage below from *Toby the Smart Dog.* Use the information from the passage to fill in the graphic organizers.

"Sit!" Nina commanded loudly and clearly. She gestured to Charlie pointing to the ground. Charlie sighed and slowly did his best imitation of an obedient, sitting dog. Nina came over to him and held out a treat. "Good boy!"

Nina praised Charlie. She clapped her hands and patted Charlie's head. Charlie pretended to chew the biscuit. Toby was starting at the biscuit. Maybe this will work, Charlie thought.

Use the information from the passage to fill in the graphic organizer.

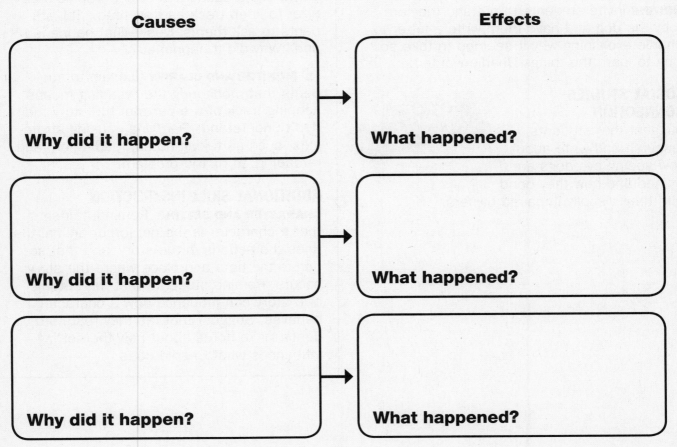

Causes

| Why did it happen? |
| Why did it happen? |
| Why did it happen? |

Effects

| What happened? |
| What happened? |
| What happened? |

Vocabulary

Directions Choose a word from the word box to answer the questions below.

Check the Words You Know		
___brightened	___commanded	___familiar
___promise	___scampered	___suspicious
___trotted	___twitched	

1. Which word describes someone getting happier? _____

2. Which word describes something that isn't quite right? _____

3. Which word describes the perky way a dog might have walked? _____

4. What word describes something you say you will absolutely do? _____

5. Which word describes how a rabbit wiggled its nose? _____

6. Which word describes something you are used to? _____

7. Which word describes someone who gave orders? _____

8. Which word describes how a mouse ran into a hole? _____

Directions Write a sentence for each of the words below.

9. suspicious

_____

_____

10. brightened

_____

_____

His Favorite Sweatshirt

SUMMARY This book tells the story of a girl who chooses to remember her brother, who is away in the U.S. Army, by continuously wearing his sweatshirt.

LESSON VOCABULARY

departure	desperately
enlisted	exhaled
garment	hesitated
neglected	resumed
superstitious	technically

INTRODUCE THE BOOK

INTRODUCE THE TITLE AND AUTHOR Discuss with students the title and cover of *His Favorite Sweatshirt*. Ask students what they think this book will be about and why it might have the title it does.

BUILD BACKGROUND Ask students what they know about the military. Ask whether anyone has had experience with a relative in the military going away from the family. Have them talk about it if they wish.

PREVIEW Explain that because this book is realistic fiction, many of the events that take place are events that could actually happen. Have students be on the lookout for traits of the main characters that make this book seem so realistic.

READ THE BOOK

SET PURPOSE Have students set a purpose for reading *His Favorite Sweatshirt*. Students' curiosity about the title or about having a relative in the military service should guide this purpose.

STRATEGY SUPPORT: VISUALIZE Tell students that by forming pictures in their minds as they read will help them understand characters, settings, and the plot. Share with students that good readers will change the picture in their minds as they read. Help students begin to visualize by recalling background knowledge.

COMPREHENSION QUESTIONS

PAGE 5 What did Carly Jean's parents seem to think about her habit of changing outfits often? *(They didn't seem to care if her clean clothes were picked up and not in the laundry.)*

PAGE 7 What made Carly Jean decide not to take over Jason's room while he was away? *(He wanted her to keep it exactly as it was.)*

PAGE 10 What prompted Carly Jean to put on Jason's favorite old sweatshirt? *(She missed him desperately; it felt like a big bear hug from him.)*

PAGE 17 What is Carly Jean's solution for keeping her sweatshirt clean? *(wear the cuffs while Mom washes the sweatshirt, then wear the sweatshirt while Mom washes the cuffs)*

PAGE 22 How did everybody find out that Jason was coming home? *(Carly told Kendra, who told Miss Wei, who told other teachers and probably their classes; parents told other parents at the bus stop.)*

PAGE 23 Try to visualize Jason's reaction to his homecoming. How do you think he reacted? *(Possible response: He was surprised and the look on his face would show his pleasure.)*

REVIST THE BOOK

READER RESPONSE

1. Possible responses:
   Carly Jean before the sweatshirt: sad that her brother is leaving for boot camp as she will be lonely
   Carly Jean after the sweatshirt: won't take it off because she is superstitious
   Both: proud of her brother.
2. Responses will vary but should include key words from text and background knowledge.
3. Possible response: People are sometimes superstitious about not stepping on sidewalk cracks, or about walking on a path a black cat has crossed.
4. Possible response: I was sad when my dad was gone for three months on a business trip. I wrote letters to him, and when he telephoned I felt better because I heard his voice.

EXTEND UNDERSTANDING Direct students' attention to page 21, where Miss Wei asks the class to adopt Jason's platoon and send letters and care packages to all of the soldiers. Explain to students that care packages are typically sent to people who are away from home for a long time—in wars, away at college, even after natural disasters like earthquakes and hurricanes.

RESPONSE OPTIONS

WRITING Have students write thank-you letters that the members of Jason's platoon might have written back to Carly Jean and other third-graders at her school.

SOCIAL STUDIES CONNECTION

Have students research the history of camouflage on the Internet or at the library. Ask them to include information about the types and patterns of camouflage.

Skill Work

TEACH/REVIEW VOCABULARY

Review vocabulary words with students. Scramble the letters of each word and invite students to unscamble the word, give its definition, and then use the word in a sentence. Have students use a dictionary if they are unsure of the meanings of any of the words.

ELL Pair students and have them create a flashcard for each vocabulary word, with a definition on the back. Direct students to go through their cards until they can state the correct definitions.

TARGET SKILL AND STRATEGY

COMPARE AND CONTRAST Tell students that *comparing and contrasting* means showing how things are alike and how they are different. Remind students that many words can offer clues to comparisons and contrasts, such as *however, different, unlike, similarly,* and *but.* Give students a topic such as "week days and weekends," and ask them to compare and contrast using clue words.

VISUALIZE Remind students that *visualizing* is forming pictures in their mind about what is happening in the story as they read. Explain to students that using their own experiences and knowledge will help them form pictures in their mind. Ask students to find any key words or phrases that helped them visualize as they read.

ADDITIONAL SKILL INSTRUCTION

DRAW CONCLUSIONS Remind students that drawing a conclusion is reaching a decision or opinion that makes sense after thinking about some facts or details. Suggest to students that as they read they think about the details and make decisions about what kind of person Carly Jean is. Have them think about other conclusions they can draw about other characters.

Name _____

Compare and Contrast

- To **compare** two or more things means to find the similarities and the differences.
- To **contrast** two or more things means to find the differences.
- Clue words such as *like, however, differently, similarly,* and *but* help you identify similarities and differences.

Directions Compare and contrast how Carly Jean felt in the beginning and end of *His Favorite Sweatshirt*. Use the chart below for your answers.

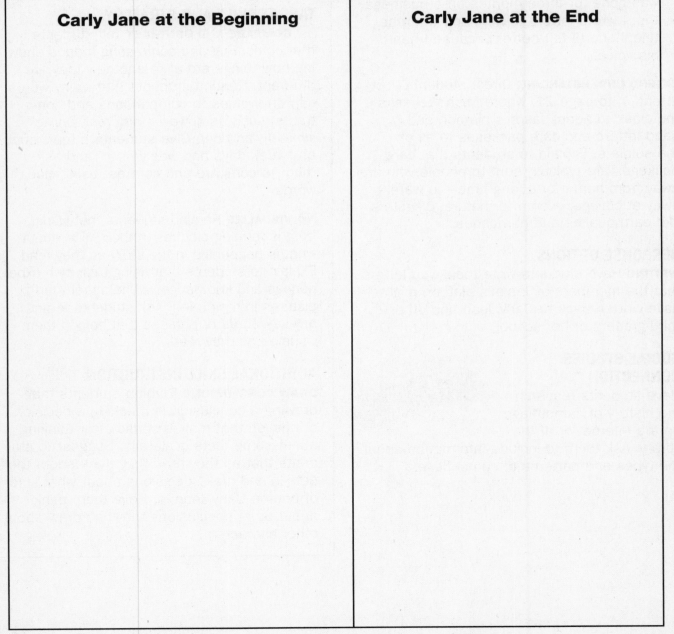

Carly Jane at the Beginning	Carly Jane at the End

94

Vocabulary

Directions Fill in each blank with the word from the word box that best fits the definition.

Check the Words You Know

___departure   ___desperately   ___enlisted   ___exhaled
___garment   ___hesitated   ___neglected   ___resumed
___superstitious   ___technically

1. signed up for a branch of the armed forces _____

2. gave too little care or attention to _____

3. believes in omens or the mysterious _____

4. any piece of clothing _____

5. began again _____

6. act of going away _____

7. in a way that is related to a specific field _____

8. failed to act promptly _____

9. breathed out _____

10. hopelessly _____

Directions Choose two words from the box and write a sentence for each one.

11. _____

_____

12. _____

_____

Life Overseas

SUMMARY This reader is about the many reasons Americans choose to live overseas for long or short periods. Their reasons are many: to work, to study, to live with another family, to serve in the military, or to volunteer. People who live abroad like to learn about other countries, languages, cultures, and customs.

LESSON VOCABULARY

abroad	ancient
anthropologists	archeologists
deployed	stationed
transferred	volunteers

INTRODUCE THE BOOK

INTRODUCE THE TITLE AND AUTHOR Discuss with students the title and the author of *Life Overseas*. Ask students to describe what they imagine this book will be about based on the title and the cover photograph.

BUILD BACKGROUND Ask students whether any of them have lived overseas. If so, have them talk about where they lived, why they were there, and how long they stayed. If there are any students who grew up in a foreign country, have them talk about what it was like for them to come to the United States. Have all students imagine where in the world they would like to live most.

PREVIEW/USE TEXT FEATURES Have students look at the headings and photographs, and discuss how these text elements help organize the book. Ask students how previewing the headings can help them understand what this book is about.

READ THE BOOK

SET PURPOSE Have students set a purpose for reading *Life Overseas*. For example, they may want to focus on the reasons people choose to live abroad. Their curiosity about foreign countries can guide them in setting their purpose.

STRATEGY SUPPORT: INFERRING Share with students the *inferring* is using information that they already know and combining it with information in the text to form their own ideas about text. Model using page 13 to make an inference about life overseas. Say: I know that college students can study abroad. I read that there are classes offered abroad that are not offered in the United States. I can infer that if a student wants to learn more about foreign topics, it would be helpful to study abroad.

COMPREHENSION QUESTIONS

PAGE 9 How does the text define what a diplomat is? *(a government worker who represents the United States abroad)*

PAGE 11 How can being an exchange student help you learn another language? *(opportunities to talk with native speakers)*

PAGE 13 How is life different for college students living abroad than for high school exchange students? *(High school exchange students live with host families while college students live in dormitories with other students.)*

PAGE 17 Are members of the military stationed overseas only during wartime? *(No, they are also stationed overseas in peacetime.)*

PAGE 18 How long do people serve in the Peace Corps? *(two years)*

PAGES 18–21 What are some of the types of work that Peace Corps workers do overseas? *(teach English, help people become better farmers, help protect the environment, help people start and run businesses)*

REVISIT THE BOOK

READER RESPONSE

1. Possible response: main idea: Reasons to live abroad Details: volunteering, Peace Corps, studying

2. Possible response: At first people in a new country would have difficulty speaking to native speakers because of language barriers. As time went on, communication would be easier.

3. Possible response: People travel a broad distance to live elsewhere.

4. Possible response: The headings clearly outlined the different reasons that people choose to live abroad.

EXTEND UNDERSTANDING Have students look through the book again, paying particular attention to the photographs. Discuss how the photos add to or take away from the meaning of the book. Have students look back at the photo on the front cover. Does that photo have new meaning now that they have read the book?

RESPONSE OPTIONS

WRITING Have students imagine that they will live abroad someday in the future. Have them pick one of the reasons in the book for living abroad. Ask them to describe where they would want to live and why. How long will they stay, and what will they do there?

SOCIAL STUDIES CONNECTION

Have students research the Peace Corps, using the library or the Internet. Have them find out how long the organization has been in existence and how many countries it has served. How many volunteers have contributed to the program? Have students find out about some of the specific projects created by Peace Corps volunteers.

Skill Work

TEACH/REVIEW VOCABULARY

Encourage student pairs to find the vocabulary words in the text. Have them define the words and then work together to write a sentence for each word.

ELL Ask students to skim the story and write down any unfamiliar words. Suggest they look up the words in the dictionary and write the meanings in their notebook.

MAIN IDEA AND DETAILS Share with students that the *main idea* is the most important idea about a topic. It can be expressed in one sentence at the beginning, middle, or end of the selection. Sometimes, however, students must figure it out and put it into their own words. Remind students that as they read, they should try to pick out the main idea and write down details that support their answer.

TARGET SKILL AND STRATEGY

INFERRING Remind students that as they read, they should think about information from the text along with what they already know. Students can use this information to form their own ideas about the text. Have students infer using pages 3, 6, and 15. *(Possible response: Many Americans move. Jobs and deployment might cause people to move overseas. There are many reasons why Americans move abroad.)*

ADDITIONAL SKILL INSTRUCTION

CAUSE AND EFFECT Remind students that an *effect* is what happened and a *cause* is why it happened. Ask: What causes people to want to live abroad? *(a desire to learn about foreign culture and language, to help others, to serve in the military)*

Name _____

Main Idea and Details

- The **main idea** is the most important idea about a reading selection.
- Sometimes it is stated at the beginning, middle, or end of the selection; but sometimes it isn't and you must figure it out yourself.

Directions Below are groups of three sentences. Write *M* next to the sentence that is the main idea and *D* next to the sentences that are the supporting details.

_____ **1.** A person takes a job overseas.

_____ **2.** Americans relocate to other countries for many reasons.

_____ **3.** People who serve in the military may be deployed to another country.

_____ **4.** Settling in new places can spark creative ideas for artists.

_____ **5.** Archeologists must move to where the artifacts can be found.

_____ **6.** Today many Americans leave the U.S. and relocate abroad for work.

_____ **7.** The Peace Corps was founded In 1961.

_____ **8.** The Peace Corps is part of the U. S. government, and it sends people overseas to volunteer.

_____ **9.** More than 178,000 Americans have participated in helping disadvantaged nations.

10. What is the main idea of *Life Overseas*?

_____

_____

Vocabulary

Directions Fill in the blank with the word from the box that matches the definition.

Check the Words You Know
___abroad   ___ancient   ___anthropologists
___archeologists   ___deployed   ___stationed
___transferred   ___volunteers

1. _____ *v.* having been assigned a station; placed

2. _____ *n.* people who study the people, customs, and life of ancient times

3. _____ *n.* people who work without pay

4. _____ *adv.* outside your country; to a foreign land

5. _____ *adj.* of times long past

6. _____ *v.* spread out troops into position for combat

7. _____ *n.* people who study human beings, especially fossil remains, physical characteristics, cultures, customs, and beliefs

8. _____ *v.* moved from one person or place to another

It's a World of Time Zones

SUMMARY Telling time is simple. What do you do if you want to know the time on the other side of the world? This book explains when and why time zones were invented, and how to use them to tell time around the world.

LESSON VOCABULARY

accurate	border
calculations	conference
horizon	observatory
rotation	solar time
standard	

INTRODUCE THE BOOK

INTRODUCE THE TITLE AND AUTHOR Discuss with students the title and the author of *It's a World of Time Zones*. Ask them to say what they think the book will be about based on the title and the cover illustration. Ask them to explain the meaning of the term *time zone*.

BUILD BACKGROUND Invite students to explain the reasons for night and day. *(earth's rotation on its axis)* Ask: When it's day here, what is it on the other side of the world? Why? Ask them if they have friends or family who live in a different time zone. Ask: What do you do if you want to call them on the phone? How do you know what time it is there?

PREVIEW/USE TEXT FEATURES Have students preview the book by looking at the photographs, diagrams, and maps. In particular, have them notice the chapter headings. Ask them to think about how the book is organized, based on the chapter headings. Ask how text features give an idea of what they will learn from reading this book.

READ THE BOOK

SET PURPOSE Have students set a purpose for reading *It's a World of Time Zones*. Students' interest in telling time and the history of establishing time zones around the world should guide this purpose.

STRATEGY SUPPORT: MONITOR AND FIX UP Have students use a graphic organizer to write down each point in the text where understanding breaks down. Have students ask a few questions at each of these points, such as "What happened first, next, and last?" Then have them continue reading.

COMPREHENSION QUESTIONS

PAGE 4 How is time measured? *(by the year, which is the time it takes Earth to make one trip around the sun; by the day, which is the time it takes Earth to complete one rotation on its axis)*

PAGE 7 Many years ago, each place kept its own time. What happened to change the way we keep time? *(In the 1800s, railroads were built and time schedules became too complicated.)*

PAGE 9 Why was the time in the town of Greenwich, England, chosen to base time zones on? *(It had an observatory that kept accurate information on Earth's rotation.)*

PAGES 10–12 Why are the world's time zones often in a zigzag pattern from north to south? *(Some countries or states moved the time zone boundaries in one direction or another so that the whole country or state would be in the same time zone.)*

PAGE 12 If you are going from Atlanta to London, how many time zones will you cross? In which direction? *(five; going east)*

PAGE 17 Where is the International Date Line? *(It runs through the middle of the Pacific Ocean.)*

REVISIT THE BOOK

READER RESPONSE

1. 1) Each town sets its own time. 2) Railroads let people travel long distances quickly. 3) People divide the world into 24 time zones at a conference in Washington, D.C.
2. Read ahead because there is more explanation on the next page.
3. border; because it's a line that separates two countries
4. Denver—2:16 P.M.; Los Angeles—1:16 P.M.; New York—4:16 P.M.

EXTEND UNDERSTANDING Have students comment on the photos and maps in the selection. Invite them to explain how the visuals help support the information presented in the text. Ask: Do you think this book did a good job of visually presenting the information? What would you have added?

RESPONSE OPTIONS

WRITING Have students work in pairs to write each other postcards from different places in the world. Have them figure out what time it is in each place as they write and explain what they have been doing. Students may wish to add a picture showing this activity on the front of their postcards. Have students exchange and read the cards.

SOCIAL STUDIES CONNECTION

Students can learn more about international time zones by visiting the library or using the Internet. They may wish to visit interactive sites such as http://nist.time.gov/.

Skill Work

TEACH/REVIEW VOCABULARY

To help students better remember the contextual meaning of *rotation,* have them reread page 4. Ask: What other words on this page help you understand the meaning of rotation? Continue in a similar fashion with the other vocabulary words.

ELL Invite students to use each of the vocabulary words in a sentence. Challenge them to compare terminology in English and in their home language.

TARGET SKILL AND STRATEGY

SEQUENCE Remind students that *sequence* means "order." Explain that clue words such as *first, then,* and *finally* are not always present to signal sequence. Invite them to look for other clues to sequence as they read. Clues include times of day and dates.

MONITOR AND FIX UP Remind students that a good reader knows that what they read should make sense. A good reader takes note of when he or she has lost the sense of the book. A good reader also has techniques or strategies for figuring out why understanding has broken down. She or he knows ways to figure out where understanding broke down in order to restore understanding. Challenge students to take note, as they read, of any point when they stop understanding the text. Suggest they improve their understanding by reviewing the sequence of events in that section before going on.

ADDITIONAL SKILL INSTRUCTION

DRAW CONCLUSIONS Remind students that a *conclusion* is a decision you reach that makes sense after you think about details or facts in what you read. Challenge students to think about the details and what happens in the selection as they read. Have them use a graphic organizer to jot down conclusions about the selection.

Name_____

Sequence

- **Sequence** is the order of events in a story.
- Authors sometimes use clue words such as **first, next, then,** and **last** to tell the order of events.

Directions Read the following statements from *It's a World of Time Zones*. Put the statements in the correct sequence in the graphic organizer below.

Train schedules made people think about time. People from twenty-five countries met at a conference in Washington, D.C., to solve the problem of telling time around the world. The countries at the conference decided to divide the world into twenty-four time zones. The railroads in the United States divided the country into four standard time zones.

1.

↓

2.

↓

3.

↓

4.

Vocabulary

Directions Read each sentence. Write the word from the word box that has the same meaning as the underlined word or phrase.

Check the Words You Know

___accurate	___border	___calculations
___conference	___horizon	___observatory
___rotation	___solar time	___standard

---

1. The four <u>normal</u> time zones are Eastern, Central, Mountain, and Pacific.

   _____

2. At a <u>meeting</u> in Washington, D.C., 25 countries created international time zones.

   _____

3. The nations of the world started with Greenwich, England, because of its excellent <u>facility for observing the movement of planets and stars</u>.

   _____

4. One day is measured by the time it takes the Earth to complete one <u>turn on its axis</u>.

   _____

5. Today, when travelers cross the <u>boundary</u> separating China from Kazakhstan, they have to set their watches ahead by four hours. _____

6. In former times, clocks and watches were not very <u>correct</u>.

   _____

7. Years ago, each town kept its own time, based on <u>the time of day as figured out by using the sun as a guide</u>. _____

8. Travelers who cross the International Date Line must use <u>steps for working out the answers to mathematical problems</u> to figure out what time they will arrive.

   _____

9. Every night, the sun sinks below the <u>western front</u>. _____

Mixing, Kneading, and Baking: The Baker's Art

SUMMARY This book describes the process of baking a variety of bread products and follows a day in the life of a baker named Claudia. On this particular day, she arrives at 2:00 A.M. and bakes rosemary bread and muffins. Soon she is ready to greet her first customer of the day!

LESSON VOCABULARY

baker's dozen	bakery
carbon dioxide	dough
fermentation	ingredients
knead	professional
recipe	yeast

INTRODUCE THE BOOK

INTRODUCE THE TITLE AND AUTHOR Discuss with students the title and author of *Mixing, Kneading, and Baking: The Baker's Art*. Ask students what they think the book will be about. Do they think baking could be considered an art?

BUILD BACKGROUND Discuss students' interest in baking. Ask if any of them have ever baked bread or watched bread being made. Have them describe the process.

PREVIEW/USE TEXT FEATURES Encourage students to look at the captions, photos, charts, and the map on page 19. How many of the international breads listed on page 19 have they eaten?

READ THE BOOK

SET PURPOSE Have students set a purpose for reading *Mixing, Kneading, and Baking: The Baker's Art*. Remind students that setting a purpose helps guide their reading. They could think about the science of baking, or a particular baked good that they enjoy.

STRATEGY SUPPORT: SUMMARIZE Draw students' attention to the two tables on pages 6 and 11. Point out that tables are graphic ways of organizing lists or steps. Students may want to make their own lists as they read. Alternatively, they can summarize the details for a section after reading it. Remind students that a good summary leaves out unimportant details.

COMPREHENSION QUESTIONS

PAGE 4 What would happen if Claudia got to work at 4:00 A.M. instead of 2:00 A.M.? *(She would be late getting started baking and wouldn't be ready to serve her customers.)*

PAGE 5 Why do bakers wear white? *(to keep the food clean)*

PAGE 6 Why do bakers use such large ovens? *(They have many things to bake at the same time.)*

PAGES 8–17 Summarize the tasks that Claudia must complete before her bakery opens. *(gets out ingredients and weighs them, makes rosemary bread, makes muffins, gets the cash register ready)*

PAGE 13 What are the names of some of the different shapes of bread? *(boule or ball, batard or torpedo, fendu or split loaf, braided loaf)*

REVISIT THE BOOK

READER RESPONSE

1. Possible response: The dough wouldn't rise.
2. Responses should give an overview of the steps listed in the chart on page 11.
3. Possible response: Bakery in center; in surrounding ovals: oven; kitchen; recipe; bread; rolls; cakes
4. Possible response: China: mooncake; Germany: pretzel; Russia: pumpernickel; Italy: focaccia

EXTEND UNDERSTANDING Have students examine the table on page 11. Ask: Is this a helpful way to list the various steps needed to bake bread? Then have students find a recipe for baking bread in a cookbook or online. Do they think they could bake bread by following that recipe?

RESPONSE OPTIONS

WRITING Have students imagine they are bakers. If they arrived at their bakery for work at 2:00 A.M., what would they bake first for their customers and then what would be baked next and so on.

SOCIAL STUDIES CONNECTION

Time For SOCIAL STUDIES

Have students research chocolate on the Internet or by using library resources. What is the history of cocoa? What are its cooking and baking properties? What countries grow cocoa beans and which countries are known for producing the finest chocolate?

Skill Work

TEACH/REVIEW VOCABULARY

Review the vocabulary words with students. What can students learn about baking from knowing the definitions of *yeast, carbon dioxide,* and *fermentation*? *(When yeast is added to dough, it eats the sugars in the dough, producing carbon dioxide, which causes the dough to rise.)*

ELL Have students describe the types of bread eaten in their home country. Have them describe the process for making bread there.

TARGET SKILL AND STRATEGY

DRAW CONCLUSIONS Remind students that to *draw a conclusion* means making a decision that makes sense after thinking about facts or details. Have students think about the following question as they read: Why does a baker need to start work so early in the morning? *(to have fresh baked goods ready to be sold first thing in the morning)*

SUMMARIZE Remind students that *summarizing* is boiling down a story to its main points. To gain practice, have students summarize their favorite books or movies. They can also take notes on the baking process as they read, and summarize the process upon finishing reading the book.

ADDITIONAL SKILL INSTRUCTION

MAIN IDEA Remind students that most stories have one or more *main ideas*. Ask students to take notes as they read, listing the main points and supporting details. Ask: What is the most important thing a baker does each day?

Draw Conclusions

- To draw a **conclusion** is to think about facts and details and decide something about them.

Directions Read the following passage from *Mixing, Kneading, and Baking: The Baker's Art*. Then write two facts about yeast and draw a conclusion.

Yeast is a tiny, live organism. It eats the sugars that are part of the dough. As it does, the yeast gives off a gas called carbon dioxide. The gas causes the dough to expand. This process is called fermentation. This process makes the bread soft and chewy.

1. Fact: _____

2. Fact: _____

3. Conclusion: _____

Directions Read the following passage from *Mixing, Kneading, and Baking: The Baker's Art*. Then write two facts about Lisa on the lines below. See what conclusion you can draw.

When Lisa comes in and orders twelve muffins, Claudia gives her an extra one for free. That's called a baker's dozen.

4. Fact: _____

5. Fact: _____

6. Conclusion: _____

Vocabulary

Directions Complete each sentence with the word from the box that fits best.

Check the Words You Know

___baker's dozen   ___bakery   ___carbon dioxide
___dough   ___fermentation   ___ingredients
___knead   ___professional   ___recipe
___yeast

---

1. When yeast is added to dough, _____ is produced.

2. The baker refused to give out her _____ for raisin bread.

3. Before beginning, the baker set out all of the _____ he would need.

4. Claudia's favorite step in the recipe was shaping the _____ .

5. The process of fermentation began after the _____ was added to the dough.

6. When Lisa ordered a dozen muffins, she got thirteen, or a

   _____ .

7. Although it can be tiring work, Claudia loves to _____ the dough.

8. The chef at the restaurant is talented and _____ .

9. When yeast consumes sugars in dough, the process of _____ takes place.

10. To buy the freshest bread, go to your neighborhood _____ early in the morning.

Let's Go Have Fun!

SUMMARY This nonfiction text explores various places to have fun. However, the information is purveyed by a fictitious character, a teacher named Mrs. Garcia. Students will learn more specific details about topics that are probably already familiar, such as skateboarding and national parks.

LESSON VOCABULARY

acrobatics	championship
exhibits	geysers
interactive	recreation
spectacular	

INTRODUCE THE BOOK

INTRODUCE THE TITLE AND AUTHOR Introduce students to the title and author of the book *Let's Go Have Fun!* Ask students what kind of information they think the book will provide based on its title. Also ask students what clues are available in the cover photograph.

BUILD BACKGROUND Ask students if they have ever gone to a state fair, and if so, what they remember about it. Also ask students if they have ever been to a national park and what they saw there. Then tell students that by reading this book, they will learn more about state fairs, national parks, and many other ways to have fun.

ELL Invite students to share a personal experience involving going someplace special to have fun. Suggest sporting events, circuses, and fairs, but explain that students do not have to limit their responses to those places.

PREVIEW/USE TEXT FEATURES Suggest that students skim the text and pay close attention to the photos and illustrations. Ask them what clues these visual elements give regarding what the book might be about.

READ THE BOOK

SET PURPOSE Encourage students to set a purpose for reading this book. Have students discuss what they would like to learn from this text based on their preview and the background discussions. They may be interested in one of the activities or places mentioned in the book. Ask them to write down two questions that they hope the book will answer.

STRATEGY SUPPORT: PRIOR KNOWLEDGE If students have prior knowledge of an activity or place mentioned in *Let's Go Have Fun!,* they are more likely to be interested in and comprehend the new material presented in the book.

COMPREHENSION QUESTIONS

PAGE 5 Is the following sentence a fact or an opinion? You can spend the whole day and night at the fair and never get bored. *(opinion)*

PAGE 7 Name four things that began at state fairs. *(cotton candy, corn dogs, butter sculptures, microwave ovens)*

PAGES 8–9 List three facts about the famous geyser, Old Faithful. *(Possible responses: It erupts about every 76 minutes. It shoots thousands of gallons of boiling water. It is in Yellowstone National Park.)*

PAGE 10 What is your favorite sport or other kind of recreation? Why? *(Responses will vary.)*

PAGE 24 Write a sentence using two of the vocabulary words. *(Possible response: A spectacular goal was made at the hockey state championship.)*

REVISIT THE BOOK

READER RESPONSE

1. to inform the reader that there are many ways to have fun, no matter where you live

2. Possible responses: Learned About: state fair, national park, Little League, skateboarding. Favorites: parties, family reunions, soccer, making jewelry

3. Possible responses: For recreation today, we went to the museum. The exhibit was spectacular.

4. Possible responses: Old Faithful is a geyser that erupts about every 76 minutes.

EXTEND UNDERSTANDING Invite students to look at the map on pages 8 and 9. Explain that maps are one type of visual aid that can help readers understand information in a text. Ask: In what part of the United States are most canyons found? *(west)* Where is the northernmost park on the map? *(Maine)* the southernmost? *(Florida)*

RESPONSE OPTIONS

WRITING Ask students to look at the map on pages 8 and 9. Then ask them to choose one national park from the map that they would like to visit someday. Have students use the Internet to do research about a state park and then write a paragraph about the features of that park.

SCIENCE CONNECTION

Geysers such as Old Faithful are unusual and fascinating natural features. Invite students to do research on the Internet or in the library to find out what makes geysers shoot hot water and steam. Ask students to find out how geysers are different from volcanoes.

Skill Work

TEACH/REVIEW VOCABULARY

Invite students to look up the vocabulary words in the Glossary. Then ask them to write a paragraph using any two of the words. Encourage students to write about their own personal experiences or to create a fictional story.

TARGET SKILL AND STRATEGY

AUTHOR'S PURPOSE Remind students that the author's purpose is the reason why the author wrote the book, and that it can be to inform, entertain, persuade, or express a mood or feeling. Invite students to discuss why they think the author wrote *Let's Go Have Fun!* Then ask students if they think the author wanted to inform and entertain.

PRIOR KNOWLEDGE Remind students that prior knowledge gathered from other books or their personal experiences can help them understand a book. Ask students if any of them have raised farm animals, skateboarded, or played on a Little League team. Have those students explain something about their activity that the other students may not know—for example, how much a horse eats or how many people are needed to make a baseball team.

ADDITIONAL SKILL INSTRUCTION

COMPARE AND CONTRAST Remind students that a comparison tells how two or more things are alike and different, and a contrast shows how two or more things are different. Words such as *like* and *as* can be clues that an author is making comparisons. Clue words such as *but* and *unlike* show that an author is making contrasts. Explain that clue words are not always used. Encourage students to ask compare/contrast questions such as "How are state fairs and Little League alike and different?" as they read this work.

Author's Purpose

- The **author's purpose** is the reason or reasons an author has for writing a story.
- An author may have one or more reasons for writing. He or she may want to **inform, persuade, entertain,** or **express** a mood or feeling.

Directions Read the following passage. Then answer the questions below.

Skateboarding is no longer what it once was. Long ago, skateboards were homemade, with roller-skate wheels attached to a plank of wood.

Now skateboarding is an entirely different ballgame! Skateboarders perform moves called *ollies, McTwists,* and *caballerials.* Watch as the skater flips, spins, and turns, and you'll see gravity at work. Gravity holds the skateboard in place with the force of nature.

1. Why do you think the author wrote this paragraph?

   _____

   _____

2. Write a fact from the paragraph that gives information about skateboarding.

   _____

   _____

3. Write a fact from the paragraph about skateboarders.

   _____

   _____

4. Do you think the author had more than one reason for writing about skateboards?

   Why do you think this?

   _____

   _____

5. Why do you think the author explains to the reader about gravity?

   _____

   _____

Vocabulary

Directions Fill in each blank with the word from the word box that best fits the definition.

> ### Check the Words You Know
>
> ___acrobatics   ___championship   ___exhibits
> ___geysers   ___interactive   ___recreation
> ___spectacular

1. underground springs that spew steam from the earth _____

2. impressive or dramatic to watch _____

3. the final stage of a sports tournament or competition _____

4. the skills or performance routines of an acrobat _____

5. allowing the exchange of information between a person and a machine

   _____

6. displays of objects of interest, especially in museums _____

7. an activity that a person does for fun _____

Directions Write a paragraph about state fairs. Use as many vocabulary words as possible.

_____

_____

_____

_____

_____

The French Connection

SUMMARY This book gives students facts about visiting places in North America that were once ruled by France. It shows how French culture can still be found in those places.

LESSON VOCABULARY

assembly line   bilingual
descendants   echo chamber
fortified   immigrants
influence   strait

INTRODUCE THE BOOK

INTRODUCE THE TITLE AND AUTHOR Discuss with students the title and the author of *The French Connection*. Ask students what they imagine this reading selection will be about, based on the title. Invite students to look at the cover photograph and discuss how this gives them more information about the selection.

BUILD BACKGROUND Discuss with students what they know about France and French culture.

ELL Invite students to discuss the parts of their cultures that they find in America, and what parts of other cultures are still in their native countries.

PREVIEW/USE ILLUSTRATIONS Suggest students glance through the photographs and map in the reading selection. Ask students which images are familiar to them and which are not. Point out the chapter headings and ask students how these help them understand what they are going to be reading about. Ask students how the photos with captioned text give the selection the flavor of someone's travel journal.

READ THE BOOK

SET PURPOSE Have students set a purpose for reading *The French Connection*. Students' interest in geography and how foreign countries influence the United States should help guide this purpose.

STRATEGY SUPPORT: QUESTIONING Share with students that good readers ask themselves questions before and during reading. Tell them that asking questions keeps them focused on the text and curious about the outcome. One example of prompting questions is to pause and think, "Does this paragraph (or idea) make sense?" of "Why did this event take place?"

COMPREHENSION QUESTIONS

PAGE 4 How did the author record her trip? What does each different recording method add to the story? *(journal writing: tells us the narrator's inner thoughts; video and postcards: give visuals and descriptions; interviews: give someone else's thoughts on the subject)*

PAGE 8 What is the main point of the paragraph about Detroit? *(Antoine de la Mothe Cadillac started a settlement called Fort Pontchartrain du Détroit.)*

PAGE 9 Why do you think the author used a series of photographs and captions in the text structure? *(The photos make it look realistic.)*

REVISIT THE BOOK

READER RESPONSE

1. Possible responses:

Facts: In 1718, the French built New Orleans. New Orleans is the only city in the United States where French was spoken for almost 100 years. The buildings in the French Quarter have tall doors that open on to lacy wrought iron balconies. Mardi Gras means "Fat Tuesday" in French.

Opinions: They must have known how important the Mississippi River would be. It is like a city inside a city. Listening to Cajun music makes me want to tap my feet! It's fun to try to catch them!

2. Responses will vary but should show understanding of text.

3. *Influence* can be used as a verb and it means "to convince." Sentence: What we read *influences* our thinking.

4. Responses will vary but should include some aspect of the following information: Elements of French culture: Quebec City: people still speak French and English; Detroit: many streets still have French names; New Orleans: has a French colonial center and Mardi Gras celebration comes from the French; St. Louis: a French name; St. Lucia: has French music, language, and food

EXTEND UNDERSTANDING Direct students' attention to the narrator, or the person who is telling the story. Ask students how the selection might have been different if there were no narrator, but just a series of facts presented instead.

RESPONSE OPTIONS

WRITING Invite students to write their own postcards from two or more of the places mentioned in the text.

SOCIAL STUDIES CONNECTION

Suggest students further research one of the places mentioned in the book. Then invite students to write and illustrate a travel brochure encouraging people to visit that place.

Skill Work

TEACH/REVIEW VOCABULARY

Review vocabulary words with students. Give students sentences with vocabulary words used correctly and incorrectly. Have students tell you whether the sentence is "true" or "false." Encourage students to correct the "false" sentences so the vocabulary word used makes sense.

TARGET SKILL AND STRATEGY

FACT AND OPINION Share with students that a *statement of fact* is something that can be proved or disproved. A *statement of opinion* is someone's beliefs and cannot be proven. It often includes clue words such as *I believe* or *in my opinion.* Remind students that a sentence can include both a statement of fact and a statement of opinion. Ask students too pick out statements of fact and opinion as they read.

QUESTIONING Tell students that good readers ask themselves questions about what they are reading to predict, understand, and find information. Model questions before reading say: I wonder what this could be about. During reading say: What does this mean? I'll read it again to find out. After reading say: I wonder where I can learn more about...

ADDITIONAL SKILL INSTRUCTION

MAIN IDEA Tell students that the *main idea* is the most important idea about of a story, passage, or paragraph. Explain to students that sometimes the author states the main idea, and other times readers must identify it and say it in their own words. Ask students to identify the main idea in *The French Connection.*

Fact and Opinion

- A statement of **fact** is one that can be proved true or false.
- A statement of **opinion** is a statement of someone's judgment, belief, or way of thinking about something.

Directions Write *F* beside statements of fact and *O* beside statements of opinion.

_____ **1.** As early as 1535, Jacques Cartier explored St. Lawrence River.

_____ **2.** Québec means "the place where the river narrows."

_____ **3.** Although Québec City is in Canada, it sure feels French to me.

_____ **4.** The Renaissance Center in Detroit is a beautiful office and hotel.

_____ **5.** Henry Ford invented the moving assembly line in 1913.

_____ **6.** The 1904 World's Fair seems like it was the place to be!

_____ **7.** St. Lucia is just twenty-seven miles long and fourteen miles wide.

_____ **8.** Cocoa, bananas, and mangoes are all grown on plantations.

Directions Read the statement: *Workers dance on the coca beans to make them easier to peel before they are shipped.* Is it a fact or an opinion? Why?

9. _____

_____

_____

_____

10. _____

_____

_____

_____

Vocabulary

Directions Unscramble the vocabulary words. Write the letter of the correct definition on the line.

Check the Words You Know

___assembly line	___bilingual	___descendants
___echo chamber	___fortified	___immigrants
___influence	___strait	

_____   **1.** gualbiiln   _____

_____   **2.** mmgistnari   _____

_____   **3.** stiart   _____

_____   **4.** fluinenec   _____

_____   **5.** blyssaem enli   _____

_____   **6.** roftideif   _____

_____   **7.** hoec hamcber   _____

_____   **8.** cendesdants   _____

a. what you are if you speak two languages

b. a thing that has effects on someone or something

c. a narrow strip of water that connects two larger bodies of water

d. people who leave one country and settle in another

e. room or space with walls that reflect sound so that an echo is made

f. made stronger against attack

g. in a factory, work passing from one person or machine to the next

h. people who are related to someone who lived in the past

China's Special Gifts to the World

SUMMARY This book describes the art and culture of China. It focuses on the ancient art of calligraphy, describing the process by which calligraphers make their own ink and study how to make the 50,000 characters in the Chinese written language.

LESSON VOCABULARY

bristles	dialects
diverse	expedition
flourished	ingredient
inspiration	literate
muffled	techniques
translation	

INTRODUCE THE BOOK

INTRODUCE THE TITLE AND AUTHOR Introduce students to the title and the author of the book. Ask students what kind of information they think this book will provide, based on the title.

BUILD BACKGROUND Discuss with students what they know about China. What do they know about the art of calligraphy? Ask students if they ever studied an art form (music, drawing) that required lots of practice.

PREVIEW/USE ILLUSTRATIONS AND CAPTIONS Suggest that students skim the text and look at the illustrations and captions. Ask students what clues these elements give them as to what this book might be about.

ELL Ask students to look at the historical map on page 4. Have them trace the trade routes and identify the countries that the routes passed through.

READ THE BOOK

SET PURPOSE Have students set a purpose for reading *China's Special Gifts to the World*. Students' interest and curiosity about China and the Chinese language can guide this purpose. As students read, suggest that they take down notes that might provide answers to any questions they have about the subject.

STRATEGY SUPPORT: INFERRING Remind students that *inferring* is using background knowledge in combination with information that they have read to create new information. Review with students what they know about China and Chinese art. Tell students to keep this in mind while they read *China's Special Gifts to the World*.

COMPREHENSION QUESTIONS

PAGE 5 How was China kept isolated from the rest of the world for so many years? *(It is surrounded by tall mountains and huge deserts.)*

PAGE 11 Read the poem by Li Po. What feeling does this poem give you? *(peaceful, calm, happy)*

PAGE 15 Look at the table. Why is it important to make all the ink you will need at one time? *(It is difficult to make two batches of ink that are exactly the same color.)*

PAGE 17 Do you think it takes longer to learn our 26-letter alphabet or 7,000 Chinese characters? *(longer to learn the Chinese characters since they need more practice)*

REVISIT THE BOOK

READER RESPONSE

1. The language is written in pictures instead of letters.
2. Responses will vary but should show understanding of the text and use of background knowledge.
3. Antonyms: *diverse,* same; *flourished,* fared poorly; *literate,* illiterate, not able to read or write, uneducated; *muffled,* clear, sharp
4. practicing to use a brush ("mo"); copying from a model ("lin"); writing your own thoughts and developing your own style ("xie")
   Responses will vary.

EXTEND UNDERSTANDING Have students research the history of our alphabet on the Internet. Can they easily read a book that was first printed in 1600? Have them imagine what it would be like to live in China and be easily able to read poems and books printed at that time.

RESPONSE OPTIONS

WRITING Imagine that you are traveling to China with the young Marco Polo in the late 1200s. Describe the things that you see, smell, and taste along the way. Describe what it is like to see Chinese writing for the first time.

SOCIAL STUDIES CONNECTION

There were many things that the Chinese developed before the Europeans. Make a list of some of the things that the book says were first invented in China.

Skill Work

TEACH/REVIEW VOCABULARY

To reinforce the contextual meaning of the word *literate* on page 6, discuss with students how the phrase *can read* helps to guess the meaning of the world *literate.* Do this with the rest of the vocabulary words in the story.

TARGET SKILL AND STRATEGY

CAUSE AND EFFECT Remind students that an *effect* is what happened, and a *cause* is why something happened. Have the students read pages 9–10. Ask: Why was the poet Li Po sent to jail?

INFERRING After reading, ask students what they have learned from *China's Special Gifts to the World.* Tell the students to take what they have learned and combine it with what they already knew about Chinese art. Explain that this will help them form new ideas about Chinese art and understand the selection.

ADDITIONAL SKILL INSTRUCTION

GENERALIZE Remind students that a *generalization* is a broad statement or rule that applies to many examples. Have students read about brushes on page 12. While the text describes some of the different kinds of brushes, what elements are common to all brushes? (*bamboo reed handle, animal hair bristles*)

Cause and Effect

- A **cause** is why something happened.
- An **effect** is what happened.

Directions Skim through *China's Special Gifts to the World* to find the text on the following topics. For each topic, list one cause and one effect.

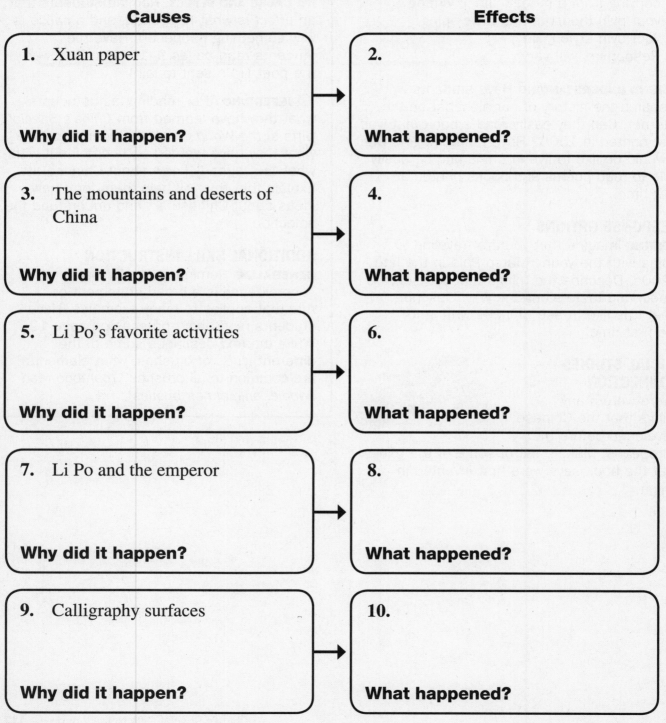

Causes

Effects

1. Xuan paper

Why did it happen?

2.

What happened?

3. The mountains and deserts of China

Why did it happen?

4.

What happened?

5. Li Po's favorite activities

Why did it happen?

6.

What happened?

7. Li Po and the emperor

Why did it happen?

8.

What happened?

9. Calligraphy surfaces

Why did it happen?

10.

What happened?

Name _____

Vocabulary

Directions Fill in the blank with the word from the box that matches the definition.

> ### Check the Words You Know
> ___bristles   ___dialects   ___diverse   ___expedition
> ___flourished   ___ingredient   ___inspiration   ___literate
> ___muffled   ___techniques   ___translation

1. _____ *v.* steadily grew, expanded

2. _____ *n.* something that stimulates a person to be creative

3. _____ *n.* the hairs on a brush

4. _____ *adj.* unable to be heard; wrapped with material to deaden the sound

5. _____ *n.* one of several substances mixed together to make a new substance

6. _____ *n.* a journey with a specific purpose

7. _____ *n.* methods of doing something

Directions Write a paragraph about China using the words *dialects, diverse, literate,* and *translation*.

_____
_____
_____
_____
_____
_____
_____

Thomas Hart Benton: Painter of Murals

SUMMARY This is a biography of American muralist Thomas Hart Benton. It supports the lesson concept of freedom of expression in a free society.

LESSON VOCABULARY

ally	appreciated
encouraged	enlisted
expression	legacy
murals	native
social	support

INTRODUCE THE BOOK

INTRODUCE THE TITLE AND AUTHOR Discuss with students the title and the author of *Thomas Hart Benton: Painter of Murals*. Explain that the book is a biography, or the real story of someone's life. Ask students to name other biographies they may have read.

BUILD BACKGROUND Discuss what students know about murals. If they have ever seen a public mural or helped create a mural, have them share their experiences.

PREVIEW/USE TEXT FEATURES Ask students to look at the table of contents. Discuss how it helps them to easily locate information in the book. Also discuss with students why each photo and art reproduction has a caption. Ask: How do the captions add to your understanding of the images and text?

READ THE BOOK

SET PURPOSE Have students set a purpose for reading *Thomas Hart Benton: Painter of Murals*. Ask students to consider the chapter titles they read in their preview. Help students by asking them to complete this sentence: I wonder _____.

STRATEGY SUPPORT: IMPORTANT IDEAS Tell students that *important ideas* are the ideas that will give readers insight into why an author wrote a selection. Explain that these ideas can be presented through headings, illustrations, or description. Model using page 5. Say: Before I read this page, I knew that an important idea would be that Thomas Hart Benton was a muralist because of the chapter title.

COMPREHENSION QUESTIONS

PAGE 5 Read the sentence, *Every school should have them.* Is it a statement of fact or a statement of opinion? Why? *(It is a statement of opinion, because it cannot be proved true or false.)*

PAGES 6–7 Do you think Benton's early childhood affected his later work as an artist? Why or why not? *(Possible response: Yes, he met many of the kinds of people he painted later in life.)*

PAGES 16–17 Why did the author include the story about Benton and President Truman? *(to inform and entertain)*

PAGE 19 Do you like Benton's paintings? Why or why not? *(Possible response: I like them because they are very colorful and lively.)*

REVISIT THE BOOK

READER RESPONSE

1. Possible response: Pictures of Benton's paintings help me visualize his work.
2. He wanted to make very large pieces of artwork. He needed a lot of space to get his ideas across.
3. Other definitions: living or liking to live with others; liking company; connected with fashionable society. Sentences will vary.
4. Responses will vary but should show comparing and contrasting.

EXTEND UNDERSTANDING Ask students to choose three photo or art reproduction captions. Have them explain the information each caption provides that is not available from viewing the illustration alone.

RESPONSE OPTIONS

WRITING Have students write a paragraph that compares the relative merits of the work of Benton and Picasso.

SOCIAL STUDIES CONNECTION

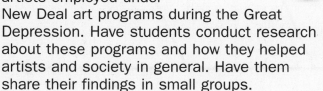

Time For SOCIAL STUDIES

Explain to students that Benton was one of many artists employed under New Deal art programs during the Great Depression. Have students conduct research about these programs and how they helped artists and society in general. Have them share their findings in small groups.

Skill Work

TEACH/REVIEW VOCABULARY

Form student pairs. Have each partner write a cloze sentence for a vocabulary word. Ask them to exchange sentences and fill in the correct word. Have students repeat the activity until all the words have been used.

ELL Make one set of cards for the vocabulary words and another set for their definitions. Have students play a memory game by pairing words and definitions.

TARGET SKILL AND STRATEGY

GRAPHIC SOURCES Tell students that graphic sources are charts or diagrams that help students understand what they have read. Have students use background knowledge to make a KWL chart. Have them fill in the first section, "What I Know," and the second section, "What I Want to Know." Suggest as students read, they fill in the last section, "What I Learned." Remind students that using a graphic organizer can help them determine the plot and the big idea of the story.

IMPORTANT IDEAS Remind students that how the text is presented can help them find important ideas and that these ideas will help the students understand why the author wrote the selection. Tell students to look at page 11 and identify the important ideas from each paragraph. Ask: How do these ideas help you understand why the author wrote *Thomas Hart Benton: Painter of Murals?*

ADDITIONAL SKILL INSTRUCTION

AUTHOR'S PURPOSE Remind students that the *author's purpose* means the author's reasons for writing. Tell students that authors often have more than one reason for writing, and that to persuade, inform, express, and entertain are common reasons. As students preview the book, ask: Why do you think the author wrote this book? *(to inform and to entertain)*

Graphic Sources

- **Graphic sources** present information visually and can help you better understand text.
- Graphic sources include chart, diagrams, maps, and pictures with captions.

Directions Fill in the sequence of events of Thomas Hart Benton's life on the time line below.

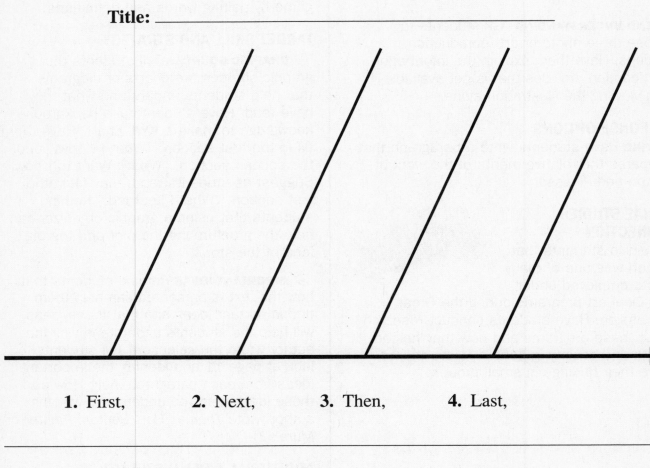

Title: _____

1. First,   **2.** Next,   **3.** Then,   **4.** Last,

_____

_____

5. How did the sequence of *Thomas Hart Benton: Painter of Murals* help you understand the story?

_____

_____

Vocabulary

Directions Draw a line from the word to its meaning.

Check the Words You Know

___ally	___appreciated	___encouraged	___enlisted
___expression	___legacy	___murals	___native
___social	___support		

1. ally   *n.* a local resident

2. appreciated   *n.* example, illustration, or demonstration

3. enlisted   *n.* backing, encouragement, help

4. encouraged   *n.* a friend or helper

5. expression   *v.* gave support to

6. legacy   *n.* large wall paintings

7. murals   *n.* a gift left by someone

8. native   *v.* was grateful for

9. social   *v.* joined or signed on

10. support   *adj.* relating to human society

Directions Using at least two of the vocabulary words above, write one statement of fact and one statement of opinion.

_____

_____

_____

_____

_____

The Best Field Trip Ever!

SUMMARY In this science fiction story, a group of nine-year-olds visits a special zoo for giant bugs. While they are at the zoo they see butterflies the size of small cars, fleas that can jump more than 150 feet, and a wasps' nest as big as a garage.

LESSON VOCABULARY

announcement	budge
entomological	exhibition
expenses	nuisances

INTRODUCE THE BOOK

INTRODUCE THE TITLE AND AUTHOR Discuss the title and the author of *The Best Field Trip Ever!* Ask students about other science fiction books they may have read. What do they think may happen in this story, based on the title?

BUILD BACKGROUND Discuss with students what they know about insects, especially butterflies. Have students ever watched a butterfly emerge from a cocoon? Have they ever collected butterflies or other insects? What is the difference between a moth and a butterfly? Have any students caught fireflies?

PREVIEW/USE ILLUSTRATIONS Invite students to look at all of the illustrations in the book. Ask students to predict what will happen from looking at the pictures. Discuss which illustrations seem realistic and which seem like fantasy.

READ THE BOOK

SET PURPOSE Have students set a purpose for reading *The Best Field Trip Ever!* They may wish to identify the fantasy elements in the story, take notes on the sequence of events, or learn more about insects.

STRATEGY SUPPORT: STORY STRUCTURE Practice with students identifying the story structure, or how a story is organized. Point out that the events in this story are chronological. Then ask students to complete a time line as they read.

COMPREHENSION QUESTIONS

PAGE 5 Who paid for the students' trip to the entomological zoo? *(The students raised their own money.)*

PAGE 7 Why was Mrs. Appleby late for the trip? *(She had been stuck in traffic.)*

PAGE 13 Where were the insects kept? *(in underground halls)*

PAGE 14 As the butterflies flew bush to bush, what happened? *(The wings sent gusts of wind that nearly blew the Bug Kids off their feet.)*

PAGE 15 Name a few of the moths and butterflies the kids saw. *(monarchs, spotted tiger moths, and pale cabbage moths)*

PAGE 18 Why were the wasps carrying food to the workers in the nest? *(to feed the larvae)*

REVISIT THE BOOK

READER RESPONSE

1. Possible responses: giant butterflies, pupas as big as soccer balls, the loud sounds of the insects, fleas that could jump more than 150 feet, giant ladybugs
2. Responses will vary.
3. Possible response: The story says that the entomological zoo is a place all about bugs.
4. Possible responses: I saw giant insects, fleas that could jump more than 150 feet, and thousands of lightning bugs.

EXTEND UNDERSTANDING Have students think about what elements of this story make it fantasy or science fiction. Have them list details from the story that describe things that could not really happen.

RESPONSE OPTIONS

WRITING Have students imagine that they found a giant butterfly in their backyard. What would they do with it? Have students imagine they could fly on the back of the butterfly. Where would they go, and what would they see?

SCIENCE CONNECTION

Have students research as much as they can find out about butterflies. Assign each student a different butterfly. They can use the Internet or the library. Have them draw a picture of their butterfly. Once they have gathered all their information, have them share it with the class.

Skill Work

TEACH/REVIEW VOCABULARY

Encourage student pairs to find the vocabulary words in the text. Have them define the words and then work together to write a sentence for each word.

ELL Have students describe their favorite insects. How do insects they may have seen while visiting or living in another country differ from insects in this country?

TARGET SKILL AND STRATEGY

PLOT AND THEME Remind students that the *plot* is the events in a story from the beginning to the middle to the end. Also, remind students that stories usually have one big idea, or *theme.* Discuss with students what they think the big idea is of familiar stories such as "The Tortoise and the Hare" (slow and steady wins the race). Have them tell the plot of the story by recalling the events in sequence.

STORY STRUCTURE Review with students that *story structure* is the way a story is organized, and that in this story the structure is chronological—events are described in the order that they happened. Remind students that understanding the story's structure can help them recognize causes and effects. Select four events from the story and write each on an index card. Give students the cards and ask them to put the events in order.neralizations about what they are reading.

ADDITIONAL SKILL INSTRUCTION

REALISM AND FANTASY Remind students that a *realistic* story tells about something that could happen. Remind them that a *fantasy* is a story about something that could not happen. As they read this story, have them think about which elements of the story are realistic and which are fantasy.

Name _____

Plot and Theme

- The **plot** is an organized pattern of events.
- The **theme** is the "big idea" of a story.

Directions Fill in the table below, which will guide you through a summary of the plot and end with your naming the theme of *The Best Field Trip Ever!*

1. Title _____

2. This story is about _____

_____

(name the characters)

3. This story takes place _____

_____

(where and when)

4. The action begins when _____

_____

_____

5. Then, _____

_____

_____

6. Next, _____

_____

7. After that, _____

_____

8. The story ends when _____

_____

9. Theme: _____

_____

Vocabulary

Directions Fill in the blank with the word from the box that fits best.

> ### Check the Words You Know
>
> ___announcement   ___budge   ___entomological
> ___exhibition   ___expenses   ___nuisances

1. We heard the _____ that blared "Put on your sunglasses!"

2. The _____ zoo was a place that was all about bugs.

3. The Bug Kids raised money to pay for their trip's _____.

4. They tried to open the door but it wouldn't _____.

5. The entomological _____ housed many gigantic insects.

6. Although insects can be fascinating, some of them can be _____.

Directions Write a brief paragraph discussing the Bug Kids' trip to the Entomological Zoo, using as many vocabulary words as possible.

_____
_____
_____
_____
_____
_____
_____
_____
_____

Free in the Sea

SUMMARY This book tells the story of a remarkable American swimmer, Lynne Cox. She showed her talent for swimming long distances when she was very young. She has not only set records for long-distance swimming, but has specialized in swimming in especially cold water, such as the Bering Strait and Antarctica.

LESSON VOCABULARY

channel	currents
endurance	fatigue
hostile	mainland
pace	pilot

INTRODUCE THE BOOK

INTRODUCE THE TITLE AND AUTHOR Discuss the title and author of *Free in the Sea*. Ask students to use the title and subtitle to explain who they think the person on the cover is and what she is doing.

BUILD BACKGROUND Explain to students that it takes special talent and training to be a long-distance swimmer, and few of those brave the icy seas that have been Lynne Cox's specialty.

PREVIEW/USE TEXT FEATURES Ask students to preview the book by checking the table of contents and paging through the book. Tell them to look at the photographs, maps, captions, and headings. Draw attention to the glossary on page 24 and invite volunteers to tell how they might use it.

READ THE BOOK

SET PURPOSE Ask students to set one or more purposes for reading, based on what they found when they previewed the book.

STRATEGY SUPPORT: INFERRING Remind students that good readers often infer, or "read between the lines," to figure out something that is not directly stated. Students can combine what they read with what they already know to make an inference about a topic or idea.

COMPREHENSION QUESTIONS

PAGES 4–5 How did Lynne's special talent show up early? *(She learned to swim as a baby and enjoyed swimming in cold water alone.)*

PAGES 6–7 What prompted Lynne to begin ocean swimming? *(Her coach discovered her talent for long-distance swimming, and Lynne discovered she loved the freedom of swimming in the ocean.)*

PAGES 8–11 What did Lynne discover about herself when she swam the Catalina Channel with her team? *(She was the fastest swimmer and could have broken the record.)*

PAGES 12–14 What set Lynne off to her specialty of long-distance swims in ferociously cold water? *(Her record-breaking swim across the English Channel.)*

REVISIT THE BOOK

READER RESPONSE

1. Responses will vary, but students may generalize that Lynne enjoyed the challenge of the dangerous swims.

2. Responses will vary, but students may infer that Lynne has such traits as courage, illustrated by her willingness to do dangerous swims; endurance, shown by her ability to swim for many hours; and generosity, shown by her attempt to bring people from different countries together.

3. Word choices and sentences will vary, but make sure students can defend their choices.

4. Responses will vary, but encourage students to be realistic as well as daring.

EXTEND UNDERSTANDING Point out to students that Lynne's body and training enabled her to carry out the swimming she did in extreme conditions. Remind students that she always had someone with her and was careful to guard her own safety.

RESPONSE OPTIONS

SPEAKING/LANGUAGE ARTS Provide books and references about some other extreme sports. Invite students to report to the class some facts about an extreme sport of their choosing.

SOCIAL STUDIES CONNECTION

Time For
SOCIAL STUDIES

Have students review and carry out the directions on pages 22–23. You may want to allow them to work in pairs or small teams. Let each team decide how to present the results of their research to the rest of the class.

Skill Work

TEACH/REVIEW VOCABULARY

Invite volunteers to read aloud the sentences they wrote with vocabulary words about Lynne Cox as directed on the Reader Response page. Then have the whole group brainstorm oral sentences that include any vocabulary word that has not been used.

ELL Explain that the word *fatigue* has come into our English language directly from French, where sometimes a word ending is not pronounced. Mention several other similar English examples with the *-gue* ending, such as *dialogue* and *catalogue*, telling students that some people now spell those two words without the final letters *ue*.

TARGET SKILL AND STRATEGY

GENERALIZE Recall with students that a broad statement that covers many different ideas is a *generalization*. Invite students to offer an example or two, perhaps about the weather. Remind students that generalizations must be supported by observable facts or statements. Ask them what facts might support their generalizations.

INFERRING Remind students that they can put together what they already know with what they read to make a decision or a generalization about something, just as they did when they considered why Lynne tried those dangerous swims.

ADDITIONAL SKILL INSTRUCTION

THEME AND PLOT Review with students that the *theme* of a story is its main idea or central meaning and that the *plot* of a story is what happens in the beginning, middle, and end of it. Point out that nonfiction, such as *Free in the Sea*, also can have a plot and theme. Challenge them to brainstorm the book's theme and to tell the events in its plot.

Name_____

Generalize

- A **generalization** is a broad statement that applies to many examples.
- Sometimes a generalization is signaled by a clue word such as *all, most, many, never, usually,* or *generally.*
- A generalization should be supported by facts and be reasonable.

Directions Think of what you know about the kind of person Lynne Cox is. Write a generalization about her. Then write several facts and statements that support your generalization.

1. Generalization about Lynne Cox

_____

_____

2. Support for the Generalization

_____

_____

_____

Directions Now think about what you learned about long-distance swimming. Write a generalization about it. Then write several facts and statements that support your generalization.

Generalization about Long-Distance Swimming

_____

_____

Support for the Generalization

_____

_____

Name _____

Vocabulary

Directions Write the word from the box that is a synonym or near synonym for each of the following words.

Check the Words You Know
___channel   ___currents   ___endurance
___fatigue   ___hostile   ___mainland
___pace   ___pilot

1. passageway   _____

2. angry   _____

3. driver   _____

4. tirelessness   _____

5. continent   _____

6. tiredness   _____

7. speed   _____

8. water flows   _____

Directions Write a paragraph that includes five of the vocabulary words in the box. Circle each vocabulary word you use.

_____

_____

_____

_____

_____

Story Prediction from Previewing

Title _____

Read the title and look at the pictures in the story.
What do you think a problem in the story might be?

I think a problem might be _____

_____

_____

After reading _____ ,
draw a picture of one of the problems in the story.

Story Prediction from Vocabulary

Title and Vocabulary Words

Read the title and the vocabulary words.
What do you think this story might be about?

I think this story might be about _____

_____

_____

After reading _____ ,
draw a picture that shows what the story is about.

KWL Chart

Topic _____

What We **K** now	What We **W** ant to Know	What We **L** earned

Vocabulary Frame

Word

Association or Symbol

Predicted definition: _____

_____

One good sentence:

_____

_____

_____

Verified definition: _____

_____

_____

Another good sentence:

_____

_____

_____

Story Predictions Chart

Title _____

What might happen?	What clues do I have?	What did happen?

Story Sequence A

Title _____

Beginning

Middle

End

Story Sequence B

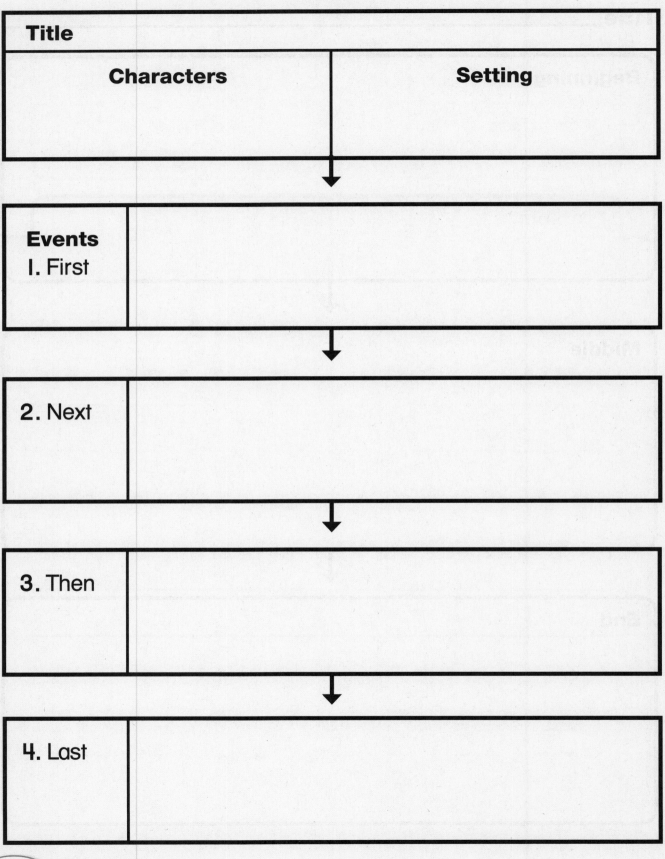

Title	
Characters	**Setting**

Events
1. First

2. Next

3. Then

4. Last

Story Sequence C

Title

Characters

Problem

Events

_____

_____

_____

_____

_____

_____

_____

_____

Solution

Question the Author

Title _____

Author _____ **Page** _____

1. What does the author tell you?	
2. Why do you think the author tells you that?	
3. Does the author say it clearly?	
4. What would make it clearer?	
5. How would you say it instead?	

Story Comparison

Title A _____

_____

Title B _____

_____

Characters	Characters
Setting	**Setting**
Events	**Events**

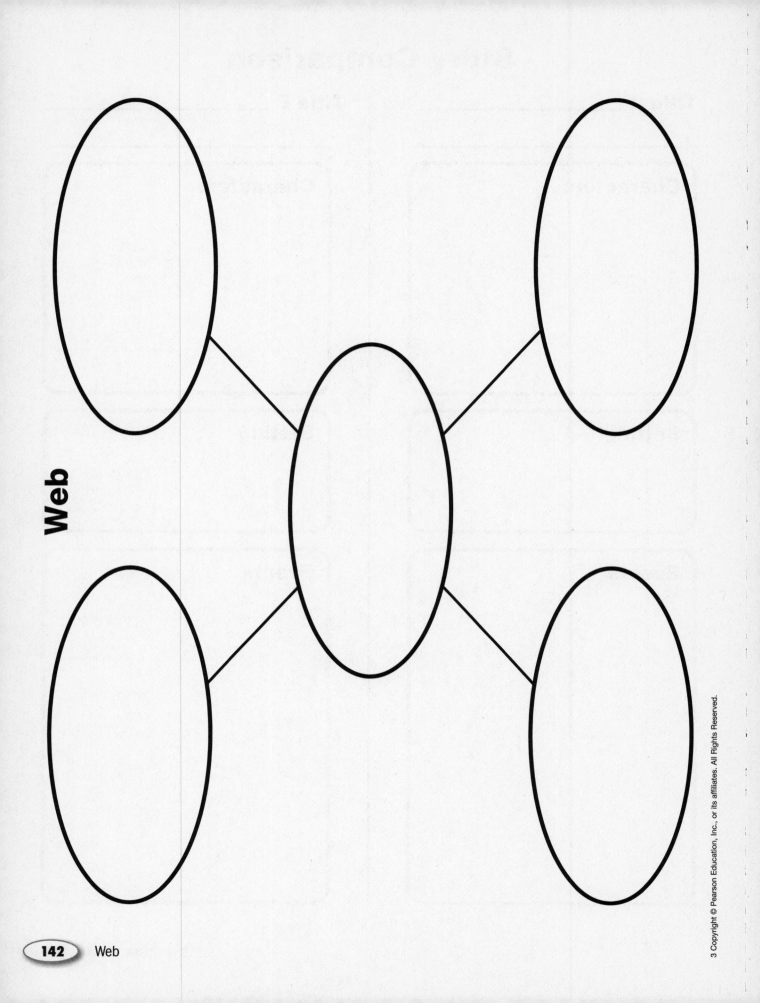

Web

Main Idea

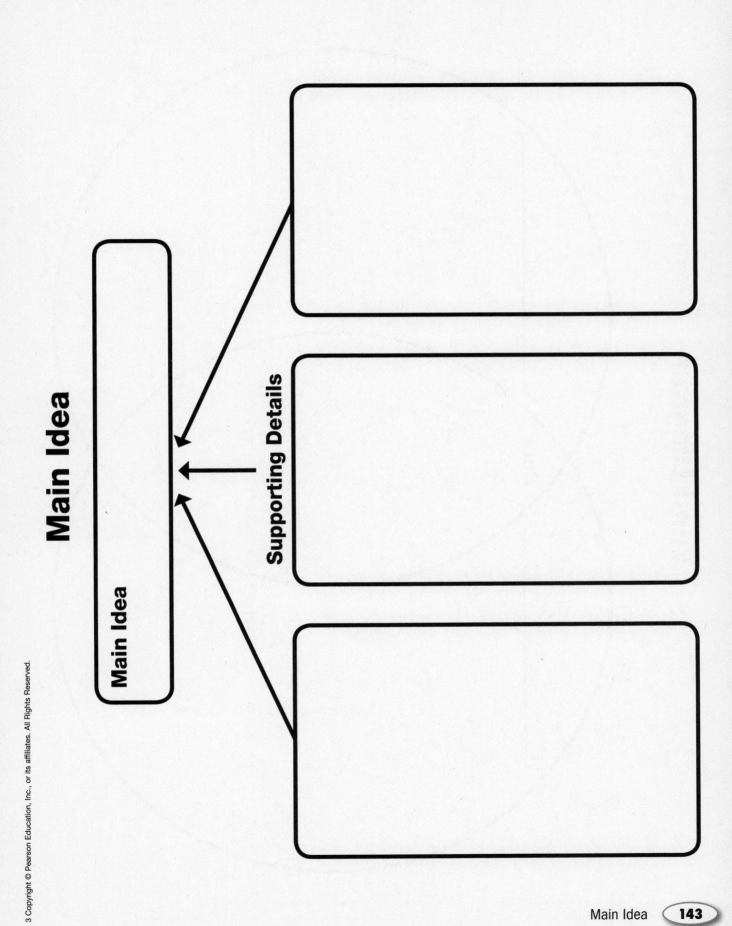

Main Idea

Supporting Details

Venn Diagram

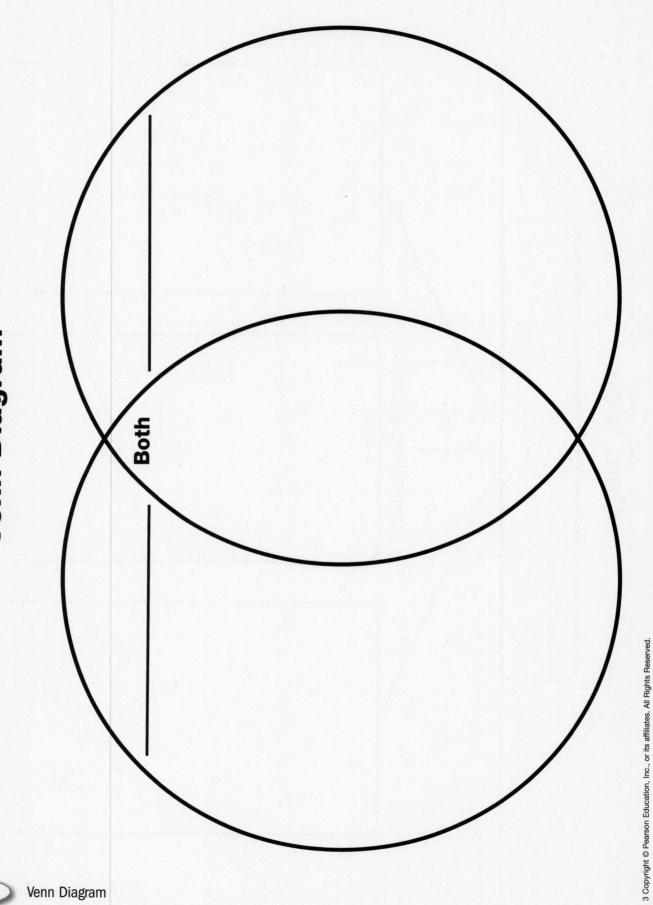

Both

Compare and Contrast

Topics

Alike

Different

Cause and Effect

Causes

Effects

Why did it happen?

What happened?

Why did it happen?

What happened?

Why did it happen?

What happened?

Problem and Solution

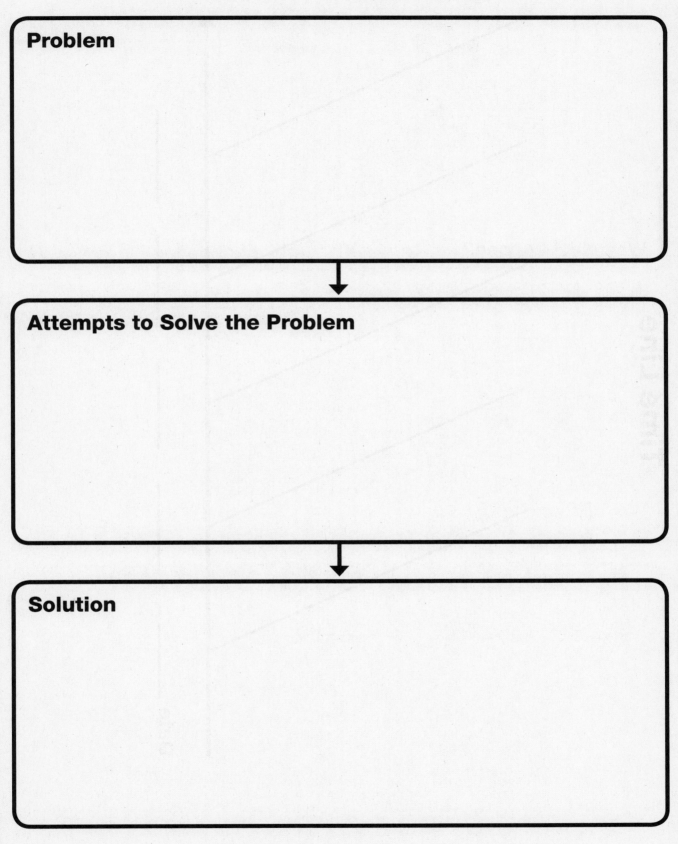

Problem

Attempts to Solve the Problem

Solution

Time Line

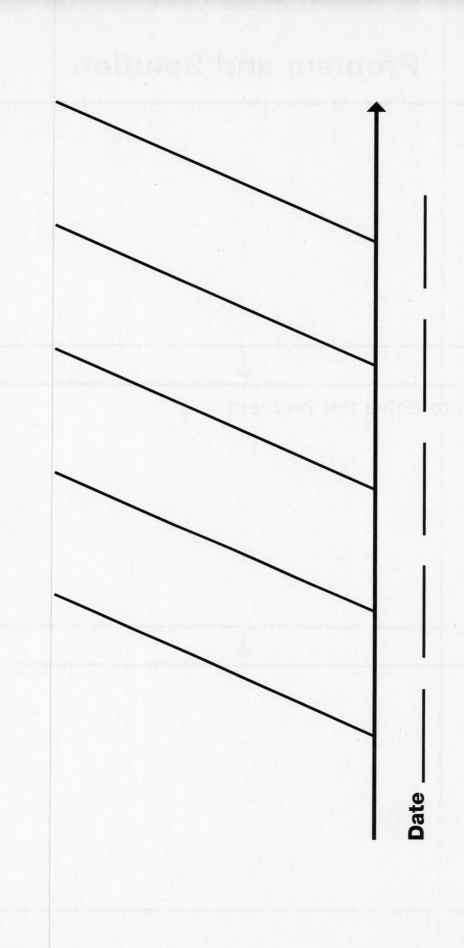

Date

Steps in a Process

Process _____

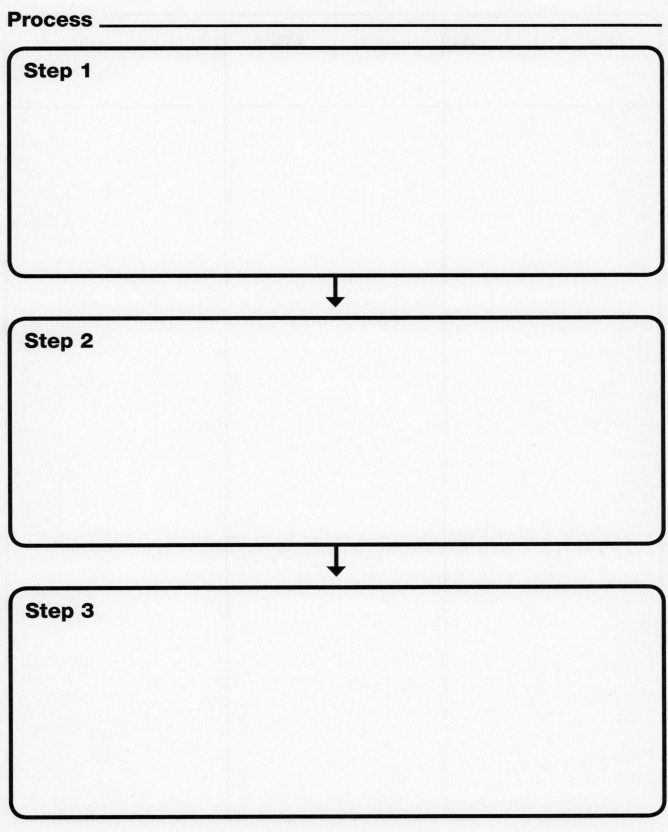

Step 1

Step 2

Step 3

Three-Column Chart

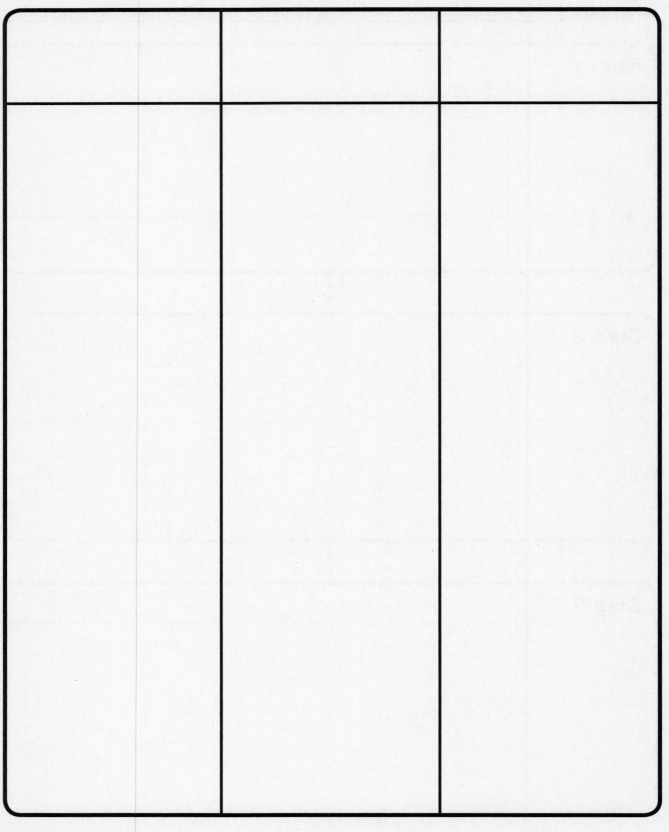

Four-Column Chart

Four-Column Graph

Title _____

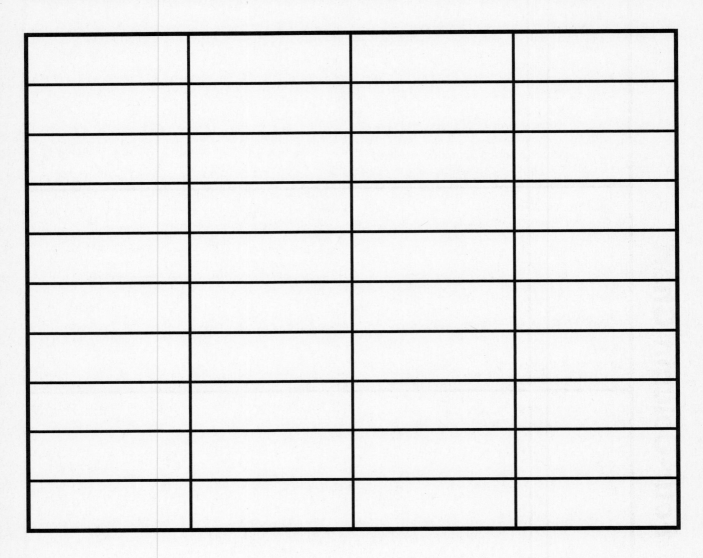

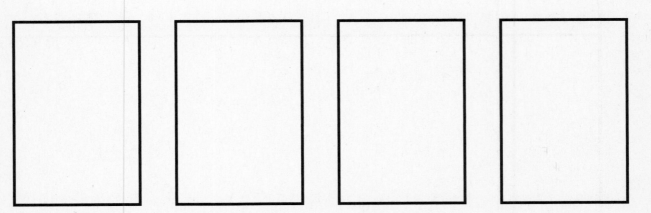

Answer Key

Leveled Reader Practice Pages

Mr. Post's Project p. 14
CHARACTER AND SETTING

Possible responses:

Trait: Mr. Post is a caring teacher; Detail: he wants to get to know each student.

Trait: Mr. Post is a good citizen; Detail: he volunteered last summer building houses.

Trait: Mr. Post is hard-working; Detail: he spends a lot of his time with the volunteer projects of his students.

Trait: Mr. Post is thoughtful/generous; Detail: he shares credit for Project Good Neighbor with his students instead of taking all the credit himself.

Mr. Post's Project p. 15 Vocabulary
1. organization
2. enthusiasm
3. volunteer
4. reporter
5. community
6. labor
7. mural
8. nonprofit
9. sign-off
10. success

Paragraphs will vary but must use vocabulary words.

What's Money All About? p. 18
SEQUENCE

Possible responses:
1. People decide what they want to trade; people bargain and/or compromise; the trade is either made or not.
2. The Egyptians sent stones, copper, grain, and papyrus to the Lebanese and received fur, cedar, and pine in return.
3. People set out what they want to trade. They decide if the trade is fair, and they take items or bring new ones.
4. First people bartered with goods. Then they used things like salt and wampum as currency. Last, people decided to use coins because they were easy to carry.
5. People were trading worldwide, and they needed a common system of money other than salt.

What's Money All About? p. 19 Vocabulary
Nouns: bargaining, compromise, currency, mints, wampum
Verbs: bargaining, compromise, mints
1. e
2. a
3. b
4. d
5. c

Journey Across the Arctic p. 22
SEQUENCE OF EVENTS

Possible responses: First, Luca and Serena hiked on snowshoes. Next, they skied to school. After that, they made an expedition to Patagonia and traveled around the world. Then, Serena found a newspaper story about two brothers making an expedition across the Arctic to the North Pole in winter. Then, they planned their trip across the Arctic. Finally, just as spring dawned, they reached the North Pole.

Journey Across the Arctic p. 23 Vocabulary
1. obstacle
2. unstable
3. efficient
4. renowned
5. lumbered
6. rigorous

Articles will vary but must use some vocabulary words.

The Road to New York p. 26
COMPARE AND CONTRAST

Possible responses: Raising Money for Double-Dutch: money goes toward a competition; your teammates can help

Both: takes a lot of hard work; you can't take no for an answer; you need to think big

Making a Movie: Money goes toward the film; your crew can help

The Road to New York p. 27 Vocabulary
1. opportunity
2. costly
3. sponsor
4. donations
5. obsessed
6. promotional
7. edit
8–10. Sentences will vary.

With a Twist p. 30
AUTHOR'S PURPOSE
1. to entertain
2. to inform
3. to express a mood or feeling

Paragraphs will vary but should show a clear purpose for writing.

With a Twist p. 31 Vocabulary
ACROSS
2. garlic
6. awnings
7. vendors

DOWN
1. ingredients
3. confused
4. oregano
5. bazaar

All About Penguins p. 34
MAIN IDEA AND DETAILS

Possible responses:
1. penguins and the Southern Hemisphere
2. The Southern Hemisphere is home to the world's penguins.
3. Penguins live on the Galápagos Islands, in Australia, New Zealand, Africa, South America, and on islands that surround Antarctica.
4. The ways emperor penguins use to reduce heat loss.
5. Emperor penguins huddle to conserve heat.

All About Penguins p. 35 Vocabulary
1. incubate
2. rookery
3. blubber
4. down
5. molt
6. brood patch
7. crest
8. lose old feathers
9. a place where groups of birds gather to raise their young
10. a layer that protects animals from the cold

Puppy Problems p. 38
COMPARE AND CONTRAST
1. Adopting a puppy or dog is compassionate.
2. You don't know the dog's background, so it may grow up as a surprise.
3. Buying a purebred dog can be expensive.
4. Because you know the dog's background, it will grow up as expected.
5. Paragraphs will vary but should include information from the story.

Puppy Problems p. 39 Vocabulary
1. abandoned
2. union
3. attachment
4. allergic
5. conference
6. apologizing
7. embarrassing
8. rally
9. Paragraphs will vary but should use vocabulary words correctly.

A Family of Collectors p. 42
DRAW CONCLUSIONS
Possible responses:
1. Fact: The cup and saucer were made in France, not England.
2. Fact: The pattern was similar to one the mother already had.
3. Conclusion: It isn't a good gift. Dad is looking for cups and saucers made in England that are unlike anything the family already has.
4–5. Facts: She had a dreamy smile on her face. It was just like her mom's face when she looks at her teacups.
6. Conclusion: Tina likes collecting just as much as her mom.

A Family of Collectors p. 43 Vocabulary
1. rim
2. credit
3. kaleidoscope
4. collectibles
5. suspiciously
6. fond
7. porcelain
8. propped
9. specialize

The Magic of Coyote p. 46
AUTHOR'S PURPOSE
Possible responses:
1. to entertain with a story of how a boy conquered his fear of dogs
2. This story informs, or explains, how humans got fire.
3. Henry likes the story about the coyote, which is similar to a dog, and it makes him less afraid of dogs.
4. She wants to inform readers about their rich tradition of storytelling.
5. Henry liked coyotes, so it was easier to like the dog part of the coydog.

The Magic of Coyote p. 47 Vocabulary
1. yelping
2. retreated
3. artifacts
4. descendant
5. cunning
6. scampered
7. breakthrough
Possible responses:
8. withdrew
9. a significant advance
10. making sharp, shrill cries or barks

Animals of the Concrete Jungle p. 50
MAIN IDEA AND DETAILS
Possible responses:
1. Alligators are common in Florida.
2. Laws helped save alligators from extinction.
3–4. Florida passed a law banning the hunting of alligators. A federal law banned shipping illegally hunted alligators across state lines.
5–7. Responses will vary.

Animals of the Concrete Jungle p. 51 Vocabulary
1. vivid
2. abundance
3. thriving
4. populous
5. loom
6. traipsing
7. emerge
8. raptors
9–10. Sentences will vary but should use vocabulary words correctly.

Grape Season p. 54
DRAW CONCLUSIONS
Possible responses:
1. All family members worked and expected to work, even at a young age. It is likely that the larger family depended on the vegetables from the garden for food.
2. Miguel's father feels trapped in his job as a grape picker.
3. Miguel's parents had never taken a vacation or gone camping, so Miguel probably wouldn't have heard of such a place.
4. Later they saw a bear scouring a picnic site looking for any food it could find.

Grape Season p. 55 Vocabulary
1. Sequoias
2. elevation
3. migrant workers
4. campsite
5. snowcapped
6. trunk
7. crop
8. trailhead

Grandmother Spider Steals the Sun p. 58
CHARACTERS, SETTING, PLOT
1. 'Possum, Buzzard, Grandmother Spider
2. Little Wasp, Fox, Wasps, people, members of the chorus, narrator
3. The place is Home and the other side of the world. The time is long, long ago before people understood the relationship between sun and Earth.
4. Beginning: People and animals lived in darkness.
Middle: 'Possum and Buzzard took turns going to the other side of the world to steal part of the sun.
End: Finally, Grandmother Spider made a pot to carry the sun and protect herself. She brought a piece of the sun to everyone. She also brought fire and taught the people how to make pots from clay.

Grandmother Spider Steals the Sun
p. 59 Vocabulary
Possible response:
1. succeed or finish; Grandmother Spider did accomplish the task.
2. a group of people singing or speaking together; The chorus chants in the play.
3. seeming to command or give orders; The narrator has a commanding voice.
4. stopped being visible; People disappeared when they had no sunlight.
5. bad luck; Buzzard had the misfortune to lose his head feathers.
6. outside edge; The person playing 'Possum in the play should go around the perimeter of the stage.
7. a search; 'Possum, Buzzard, and Grandmother Spider all went on a quest for the sun.

Animal Tracking: Learn More About Animals p. 62
GRAPHIC SOURCES
Ways of Tracking: Radio and GPS collars, dressing as birds, airplanes, teaching whooping cranes to migrate.
1. Responses will vary but should show an understanding of text structure.

Animal Tracking: Learn More About Animals
p. 63 Vocabulary
1. a; someone who studies life
2. a; to spend the winter in slowed-down, sleeping condition.
3. a; information
4. a; living creature who feeds its young milk, has hair on its body, and does not lay eggs
5. b; to look at something critically

Whales and Other Amazing Animals p. 66
GENERALIZE
Possible responses:
1. Some get stuck in marsh grass in a bay.
2. Some get trapped in narrow channels.
3. Today's large ships use noisy propellers.
4. Sonar may disrupt whales when they echolocate.
5. With fewer wolves, the number of coyotes increases.
6. More coyotes mean less food for hawks.
7. Both warn people about dangers by barking.
8. Both protect people.
9. Wahoe, a chimpanzee, can "speak" using sign language.
10. Koko, a gorilla, has two cats as her pets.

Whales and Other Amazing Animals
p. 67 Vocabulary
1. f
2. h
3. b
4. d
5. g
6. a
7. e
8. c
Paragraphs will vary but should use at least three vocabulary words.

Coral Reefs p. 70
CAUSE AND EFFECT
Possible responses:
1. because they don't have the hard outer skeletons that make up the reefs
2. because soft corals do not need as much sunlight
3. because something has made it need to protect itself
4. because coral can only live in warm water
5. Responses may vary but may include dynamite fishing, using poison to catch fish, pollution, global warming, tourists, building too close to shore.
6. Responses may vary but may include creating marine parks, planting mangrove trees and other plants, reducing global warming, supporting groups that protect the reefs, keeping trash out of the ocean, and conserving water.

Coral Reefs p. 71 Vocabulary
1–7. Sentences will vary but the use of a context clue should show an understanding of the vocabulary words.
8. Sentence will vary but should use a minimum of two vocabulary words.

Extraordinary Athletes p. 74
GENERALIZE
Possible responses:
1. Disabled athletes generally work harder than others to achieve in their sports.
2. Jean Driscoll towed other athletes behind her when she was training. Oscar Pistorius learned to run so fast that he beat non-disabled athletes. Erik Weihenmayer had to learn to climb mountains by relying on his other senses, since he had no sight.
3. Events such as the Paralympics and the Boston Marathon offer disabled athletes a chance to compete against people with similar disabilities.
4. The Paralympics are special games for athletes with disabilities. The Boston Marathon has divisions for both runners and wheelchair racers.

Extraordinary Athletes p. 75 Vocabulary
1. summit
2. amputated
3. marathon
4. disabilities
5. advantage
6. determination
7. amputated, qualified, ultimate
8. disabilities
9. amputated, qualified
10. advantage, marathon, qualified, ultimate

Largest, Fastest, Lightest, Longest p. 78
GRAPHIC SOURCES
Possible responses:
1. The grouse was faster, according to the illustration.
2. that copies of the *Guinness World Records* have been printed and sold
3. It shows the location of the place on a map with clouds and rain and a caption that tells the information we are supposed to know from the text.
4. the largest number of tap dancers dancing at once
5. Guinness receives about 60,000 forms every year.

Largest, Fastest, Lightest, Longest p. 79 Vocabulary
1. trivia
2. compendium
3. verified
4. accomplishment
5. procedure
6. verified
7. superlative
8. accomplishment
9. translated
10. existing

Gemstones Around the World p. 82
FACT AND OPINION
1. Fact
2. Fact
3. Opinion
4. Fact
5. Opinion
6. Fact
7. Fact
8. Opinion
9. Fact
10. Fact

Facts can be checked in books, by observing, or by asking an expert. Opinions are personal judgments.

Gemstones Around the World p. 83 Vocabulary
1. crystal
2. brilliant
3. transparent
4. flaws
5. rockhounds
6. birthstone
7. quartz
8. mined

Changing Times: Women in the Early Twentieth Century p. 86
FACT AND OPINION
1. In 1920, a new law gave women the right to vote.
2. Most women did not mind working at home. This statement is the author's belief or opinion about women and cannot be checked.
3. Oberlin College opened its doors to both men and women in 1833.
4. Of course, it was not easy for these women.
5. Fact: Many women choose to stay home. Opinion: The most important job of all is being a mother.

Changing Times: Women in the Early Twentieth Century p. 87 Vocabulary
Possible responses:
1. prejudice, -ed, Martin Luther King, Jr., fought against *prejudice*.
2. criticize, -ed, People should not *criticize* each other's clothing.
3. accept, -ed, Sometimes you have to accept the outcome for something you did.
4. opportunity, -ies, I took the *opportunity* to go to the amusement park on a free pass.
5. limit, -ed, It is a good idea to try to *limit* how much chocolate you eat.

Diary entries will vary.

Toby the Smart Dog p. 90
CAUSE AND EFFECT
Possible responses:
Cause: "Sit!" Nina commanded. **Effect:** Charlie did his best imitation of an obedient, sitting dog. **Cause:** "Good boy"! Nina praised Charlie and she clapped her hands and patted Charlie's head. **Effect:** Charlie pretended to chew the biscuit. **Cause:** Toby was staring at the biscuit. **Effect:** *Maybe this will work,* Charlie thought

Toby the Smart Dog p. 91 Vocabulary
1. brightened
2. suspicious
3. trotted
4. promise
5. twitched
6. familiar
7. commanded
8. scampered
9–10. Sentences will vary.

His Favorite Sweatshirt p. 94
COMPARE AND CONTRAST
Possible responses:
Beginning: Sad, worried, or concerned.
End: Supportive, excited, or happy

His Favorite Sweatshirt p. 95 Vocabulary

1. enlisted
2. neglected
3. superstitious
4. garment
5. resumed
6. departure
7. technically
8. hesitated
9. exhaled
10. desperately
11–12. Sentences will vary.

Life Overseas p. 98

MAIN IDEA AND DETAILS

1. D
2. M
3. D
4. D
5. D
6. M
7. D
8. M
9. D
10. Why Americans live abroad.

Life Overseas p. 99 Vocabulary

1. stationed
2. archeologists
3. volunteers
4. abroad
5. ancient
6. deployed
7. anthropologists
8. transferred

It's a World of Time Zones p. 102

SEQUENCE

1. Train schedules made people think about time.
2. People from twenty-five countries met at a conference in Washington, D.C., to solve the problem of telling time around the world.
3. The countries at the conference decided to divide the world into twenty-four time zones.
4. The railroads in the United States divided the country into four standard time zones.

It's a World of Time Zones p. 103 Vocabulary

1. standard
2. conference
3. observatory
4. rotation
5. border
6. accurate
7. solar time
8. calculations
9. horizon

Mixing, Kneading, and Baking: The Baker's Art p. 106

DRAW CONCLUSIONS

Possible answers given.
1. Yeast eats the sugars in the dough.
2. Yeast gives off carbon dioxide.
3. Yeast causes dough to rise.
4. Lisa orders 12 muffins.
5. Lisa receives 13 muffins.
6. A baker's dozen equals 13 muffins.

Mixing, Kneading, and Baking: The Baker's Art p. 107 Vocabulary

1. carbon dioxide
2. recipe
3. ingredients
4. dough
5. yeast
6. baker's dozen
7. knead
8. professional
9. fermentation
10. bakery

Let's Go Have Fun! p. 110

AUTHOR'S PURPSE

Possible responses given.
1. to inform about skateboarding
2. Skateboards used to be homemade.
3. They flip, spin, and turn on their boards.
4. yes, to inform and to entertain
5. to give information

Let's Go Have Fun! p. 111 Vocabulary

1. geysers
2. spectacular
3. championship
4. acrobatics
5. interactive
6. exhibits
7. recreation

Paragraphs will vary.

The French Connection p. 114

FACT AND OPINION

1. F
2. F
3. O
4. O
5. F
6. O
7. F
8. F
9. Opinion.
10. This statement contains a feeling or belief.

The French Connection p. 115 Vocabulary

1. a, bilingual
2. d, immigrants
3. c, straits
4. b, influence
5. g, assembly line
6. f, fortified
7. e, echo chamber
8. h, descendants

China's Special Gifts to the World p. 118

CAUSE AND EFFECT

Possible responses:
1. It doesn't tear easily and resists insects.
2. Artwork on Xuan paper has lasted a long time.
3. China has huge mountains and deserts.
4. They long kept China isolated from Europe.
5. Li Po loved nature, friends, and time alone.
6. He often took time off for "wandering."
7. The emperor thought Li Po wanted to create a new kingdom.
8. He had Li Po sent to jail.
9. Calligraphers can paint their characters on any surface.
10. Some artists draw on silk.

China's Special Gifts to the World p. 119 Vocabulary

1. flourished
2. inspiration
3. bristles
4. muffled
5. ingredient
6. expedition
7. techniques

Responses will vary.

Thomas Hart Benton: Painter of Murals p. 122
GRAPHIC SOURCES
Possible responses:
Title: Thomas Hart Benton
1. First, Thomas spent his childhood traveling to many places with his political family.
2. Next, Thomas made his big break in New York City.
3. Then, Thomas became famous and met many important people.
4. Last, Thomas is remembered for his honest depiction of American history.
5. Responses will vary but should show understanding and use of text structure.

Thomas Hart Benton: Painter of Murals p. 123
Vocabulary
1. *n.* a friend or helper
2. *v.* to be grateful for
3. *v.* joined or signed on
4. *v.* gave support to
5. *n.* example, illustration, or demonstration
6. *n.* a gift left by someone
7. *n.* large wall paintings
8. *n.* a local resident
9. *adj.* relating to human society
10. *n.* backing, encouragement, help
Statements will vary but should clearly state fact and opinion.

The Best Field Trip Ever! p. 126
PLOT AND THEME
1. The Best Field Trip Ever!
2. the Bug Kids (Emma, Jacob, Kayla, Luke, Carlos, and Lily), Mr. Edwards, Mrs. Appleby, and Elvis.
3. at the school and at the Entomological Zoo
Possible responses:
4. The Bug Kids take off in the school van for the zoo. They spend one night in the Butterfly Lodge.
5. They see butterflies that are unbelievably huge.
6. They see wasps and cicadas, which are also huge.
7. They see fleas that can jump 150 feet.
8. They return home.
9. Possible theme: One should respect insects.

The Best Field Trip Ever! p. 127 Vocabulary
1. announcement
2. entomological
3. expenses
4. budge
5. exhibition
6. nuisances
Paragraphs will vary.

Free in the Sea p. 130
GENERALIZE
1. Responses may vary but should reflect the content of the story.
2. It is clear that Lynne likes dangerous swims from the many examples of the ones she has carried out.
Generalization: Responses will vary but should reflect the content of the story. For example, students may generalize that long-distance swimming takes a great deal of training as well as talent.
Support: Lynne spent years training for her record-breaking swims.

Free in the Sea p. 131 Vocabulary
1. channel
2. hostile
3. pilot
4. endurance
5. mainland
6. fatigue
7. pace
8. currents
Responses may vary. Make sure students use the vocabulary words correctly.